Salomon Jadassohn

Manual Of Musical Form

Salomon Jadassohn

Manual Of Musical Form

ISBN/EAN: 9783742810601

Manufactured in Europe, USA, Canada, Australia, Japa

Cover: Foto ©Angelika Wolter / pixelio.de

Salomon Jadassohn

Manual Of Musical Form

MANUAL

OF

MUSICAL FORM

BY

Dr. S. JADASSOHN,

PROFESSOR AT THE ROYAL CONSERVATORIUM OF MUSIC, LEIPZIG.

TRANSLATED FROM THE GERMAN

BY

E. M. BARBER.

THIS WORK IS COPYRIGHT.

BREITKOPF AND HÄRTEL

LEIPZIG, BRUSSELS, LONDON, NEW YORK.

1892.

AUTHOR'S PREFACE.

The translation of my "Formenlehre" has been undertaken by my highly-gifted dear friend and former pupil, Mr. Edwin Barber, at my special wish and under my personal supervision.

Several examples not contained in the German, with the necessary explanations have been added to the English translation. I gladly take this opportunity of thanking Mr. Barber for the care he has bestowed upon my work.

LEIPZIG, March 13, 1892.

Dr. S. JADASSOHN.

TRANSLATOR'S PREFACE.

In translating this work, I have endeavoured to employ the correct terminology as far as our language would permit, introducing no terms which have not been previously made use of by the best English writers on this subject.

I trust the book will receive that attention from the student which the Author's opinions merit. In conclusion I wish to thank Dr. Jadassohn for his kind and ready assistance.

LEIPZIG, March 14, 1892.

E. M. BARBER.

PREFACE.

The present treatise is intended to offer a helping hand to the student in his efforts to study and analyse the works of the classical masters, and at the same time to act as a guide for his own practical work. A clear knowledge of musical form must be first acquired before the realms of composition can be entered.

As the pupil's acquaintance with musical literature is at first usually small and limited, I have only referred to a few works and those, such as are generally well-known and easily obtainable. I have especially selected my examples in the majority of cases from Beethoven, for we have to thank this master for the more perfect construction of modern musical form. An enlarged introduction, a broader Free Fantasia, an extended Coda, the entry of the second subject in the key of the mediant in the first part of a Sonata in a major key, the addition of the Scherzo in the Sonata, its double repetition as well as that of its accompanying Trio, not to mention many other facts to which the attention of the pupil is drawn in this work: these are the acquisitions, for the possession of which all later composers are indebted to Beethoven. Moreover his works are to-day still the most popular.

By numerous musical examples and additional explanation, I have endeavoured to make this work perfectly clear and serviceable for self-instruction.

TABLE OF CONTENTS.

                                                                    Page

Chapter I. The development of Melody   1
    § 1. Different Kinds of Melody, the Motive.
    § 2. Longer Motives, the Period.
    § 3. Formation of Melody by Combination of Periods.
    § 4. Formation of the Close of a Melody.

Chapter II. Song and Simple Song-Form   25
    § 5. The Melody of a Song.
    § 6. Songs in which each Verse is set to the same Music.
    § 7. Simple Song-Form in Instrumental Music.

Chapter III. Variation-Form   41
    § 8. Different Kinds of Variations.
    § 9. The Subject.
    § 10. More important Variation-Forms.
    § 11. The Close of the Variations.
    § 12. Free Variation-Form.

Chapter IV. Dance-Form   53
    § 13. The Contrasted Movement.
    § 14. Protracted Dance-Form.

Chapter V. The protracted, combined Song-Form   65
    § 15. The Song with different music to each verse, the Ballad, the Aria, Arietta, Arioso, Cavatina, Romanza, Scena and Aria, Chorus in Opera and Oratorio.
    § 16. Protracted Song-form in Instrumental Music.

Chapter VI. Rondo-Form   77
    § 17. The Rondo without Episode of Contrast.
    § 18. The Rondo with Episode of Contrast.

Chapter VII. The Sonata   87
    § 19. The Form of the Sonata in general.
    § 20. Different Arrangements of the several movements.

	Page
Chapter VIII. The Sonatina	92

§ 21. The First Movement in a major key.
§ 22. The First Movement in a minor key.

Chapter IX. The First Movement of a Sonata 109
§ 23. The first Part of the First Movement; the first Subject and its connection with the second.
§ 24. The Modulation after the first Subject.
§ 25. The second Subject.
§ 26. The Coda in the first Part.

Chapter X. The Second Part of the First Movement   128
§ 27. The Free Fantasia.
§ 28. Various Commencements of the Free Fantasia.

Chapter XI. The Third Part of the Movement and the Extended Coda; the Remaining Movements of a Sonata . . . 138
§ 29. The Key of the second Subject in the third Part.
§ 30. Contraction of the first Subject in third Part.
§ 31. The Extended Coda.

Chapter XII 148
§ 32. The Prelude, Etude, Capriccio, Fantasia, Suite, Overture, Variations in the Form of a Sonata-Movement.
§ 33. The Concerto.

CHAPTER I.

THE DEVELOPMENT OF MELODY.

Different Kinds of Melody, the Motive.

§ 1. Every musical composition, be it ever so small, must contain one musical idea. This is called the Subject. Most works contain, as a rule, more than one Subject; and we shall find in studying the more highly developed compositions, such as Sonatas and Symphonies, that besides the two chief Subjects, other musical ideas will be necessary, in part to connect the Subjects and in part to form a conclusion to a movement, or the part of a movement. A complete movement can be developed from one single subject, as for instance in an air with variations.

The Subject of a composition should always be a rhythmically and metrically constituted melody; for we hear and we perceive it, even where it cannot be readily distinguished owing to its manifold adornments, as in many Preludes and Studies. In proof of this assertion let us turn to the first prelude in Bach's Wohltemperirte Clavier and the first Etude of Chopin, op. 10. Although in both these pieces an harmonic succession is only apparently given, still in both we hear the melody above the broken chords, without its being especially marked as in Chopin's Study op. 25. I.

We distinguish two different kinds of melody; firstly such as are constructed upon an initial figure, secondly such as those which contain a figure, and make use of this in their progression, to assist the formation of the melody as a whole, but are still not strictly developed from an initial figure. As an example of the former we give the first subject of Beethoven's Overture to Coriolanus:

This example requires no further explanation than that the Subject is a development of the figure:

As an example of the second species we would suggest the commencement of Schubert's Symphony in C:

In this case, the rhythmic figure of the second bar is made use of in the third, fifth, and sixth bars for the formation of the melody; the augmentation of the figure in the seventh bar, as a preparation for the close.

We also find melodies in which there are no traces of the use of a figure for the purpose of development, and we give as an example the subject of the Adagio from the Sonata pathétique:

Different Kinds of Melody. the Motive. 3

This species is however most rarely to be met with, being generally found in songs and sustained slow movements of a cantabile nature. Should we come across these in a quick tempo, they still retain the character of a slow sustained song-melody. Compare the first Cantilene in Chopin's B♭ minor Scherzo, the first subject of Beethoven's Sonata, op. 28, (first movement), and the subject of the Andante in the same.

Melodies developed from figures, on the other hand, alike in quick and slow time and both in works of long and short duration are abundant. We must therefore give our attention in the next place to the Figure or Motive which we must regard to some extent as the germ of the Subject. This germ, the motive, can be so small, meagre and insignificant, that we are unable to recognise the key or the division of the bar in which the melody shall be formed. At times the figure or motive does not even complete a whole bar, as in Beethoven's Sonata op. 31. II:

The Development of Melody.

4 a.

If we hear this figure alone, we are unable to say whether it is in duple or triple time, and the accent alone decides whether it begins on the strong or the weak beat — thus:

4 b.

Only by the repetition of the same figure in the second bar are we assured of the movement being in $\frac{3}{4}$ time. Even then the key is not settled, for the chord in question can equally belong to the key of E♭ major (second degree) or the key of C minor (fourth degree) as a $\frac{6}{4}$ chord. But even overstepping the bar-line, and proceeding two bars further the listener is still left in doubt alike as to key and tempo, not only by the imitation of the rhythmic parts but also by the melodic design of this imitative figure. The motive of the first movement of Beethoven's Symphony in C minor leaves the audience in doubt whether, what he hears in the first four bars, is written in E♭ major or C minor, and further whether it is in duple or triple time*).

---

*) The initial figure of the Rondo from Beethoven's Sonata op. 10 No. 3 suggests neither key nor rhythm, when quoted thus:

4 c.

The motive derives its most individual characteristics from the rhythm it contains. At the commencement of the A major Symphony, Beethoven gives the marked rhythm of the movement at first only upon E. This rhythm is to be found alike in the first and second subjects of the movement and gives to the whole its spirited motion. Schumann's Symphony in B♭ major, begins with the motive which in the allegro movement is employed in diminution for the structure of the first subject. This motive extending only over the three notes which form the interval of the major third, distinguishes only the rhythm and not the key of the subject, for the structure of which it is employed later. So far as the melodic design is concerned the motive could just as well belong to G minor as B♭ major.

The motives which we have so far ventured to suggest, are isolated instances. In general, even with the very shortest motives which are formed of a few notes, the key of the movement is clearly defined. The following short motives

Bach, wohlt. Cl., Fuge II.

Beethoven, Sonata II.
Allegretto.

Beethoven, op. 22.
Allegro con brio.

Beethoven, op. 31, Nr. 2.
Allegretto.

leave no one in doubt as to the key; but longer motives, especially a repetition or imitation through several bars, leave the hearer in doubt over the rhythm of the subject if the performer does not give certain hints by his accentuation. Beethoven begins his Sonata, op. 14, No. 2, in the following manner:

Unless they were made aware of the strong beat of the first bar by the accent of the performer, the audience would in this case surely hear the subject with the following false rhythm for the first four bars, and not become aware of their mistake until the fifth.

Should the performer display the unskillfulness (no uncommon occurrence), of accenting in the least degree the highest note of the motive, which moreover, because it is the highest, occurs most frequently, the hearer would conceive the first bars of the subject as follows:

There are circumstances under which the rhythm of the motive can be correctly enunciated, and even if the motive and repetition form two whole bars the division of the bar in which the subject is written, remains a doubt to the listener. The last movement of the above-mentioned Sonata presents a striking instance of this in its initial bars.

The audience in this case only become aware in the third bar that the subject is not in duple

but in triple time. The rhythm of the motive suggests duple time most distinctly from its threefold imitation within the first bars.

In most cases however the key of the subject as well as the division of the bar, in fact the whole movement would be clearly defined by the repetition of the initial figure or its imitation in the second bar.

14.

In the previous example any doubt of the key would be set aside at the very commencement by the harmonies of the accompaniment. We add yet one more example in which the key and the division of the bar are alike assured not only by the strict repetition of the notes but by the imitation of the motive; it is the beginning of Beethoven's Rondo op. 49. I.

15.

Even without the additional accompaniment both the key and tempo of the movement can be safely recognised owing to the imitation of the motive in these two bars.

Longer Motives, the Period.

§ 2. We have so far only dealt with the shortest motives, which either do not occupy a whole bar, as in Ex. 4, or which complete the bar as in the first bar of Ex. 1, or with such as extending beyond the bar-line, do not form a complete bar in the sum total of their notes, as in Ex. 12, or finally with those which extending also beyond the bar-line, yield in the sum of their notes a complete bar, as in Exs. 9 and 15. Only in such cases can there be an occasional doubt as to the key and time; as a rule however key and time are alike distinct in such short motives. In longer motives which occupy the space of two bars in part or completely, be they filled with notes or rests both key and time are distinctly visible in the motive. We add some of the latter kind of motives; under Exs. 16 and 17 such as do not complete two bars.

Under Exs. 18 and 19 we find motives in which two whole bars are completed by means of rests.

In conclusion we give two motives whose rhythmical constituent parts form exactly two bars.

The Development of Melody.

We also find motives which, extending over several bars, form the antecedent section of a period of a melody; thus:

In this case we have to deal with a combination of two motives, which "dovetail" so to speak, and of which the close of the former is coincident with the commencement of the latter.

Both motives occur in the first movement of Beethoven's C minor Concerto and are employed both as a whole and separately. The second motive which is given out by the drums towards the close of the movement, forms a most interesting organ point.

Furthermore we would prove to the pupil how the melody, the subject of the movement, can be developed and formed from the motive. Each subject of a composition in the free style must be a rhythmically and metrically constituted whole. A metre is a part of period whose antecedent or relative sections, and in some cases the middle section, form and to a certain extent give a hiatus or Cæsura to the melody; the metre of music is measured by bars just as the metre of verse is regulated by syllabic feet. The smallest period in two-bar metre is at least four bars long, in four-bar metre eight bars; it may terminate with a full close or a half close on the dominant. We find a four-bar metre, formed by means of a repetition of the motive, in Beethoven's Sonata op. 31. III; a two-bar metre, similarly developed, in Chopin's Impromptu in A flat major; whilst in the former master's Sonata op. 49. II, we have the same effect produced by a transposition to the higher octave. Chopin's Scherzo in B flat minor, op. 31, constitutes a fine example of extended four-bar metre; the first twenty-four-bar period repeating almost exactly, makes in all a forty-eight-bar melody. The student will also find examples of four and two-bar metres by referring to Beethoven's op. 31. II, and further, illustrations of four and three-bar metres in the ninth symphony of the same master. If we look at the Volkslied "Fahret hin Grillen", we shall see that both the antecedent and relative section of the period end on the chord of the tonic.

A contrast in the metre is beautifully illustrated in the second subject of the first movement of Beethoven's Sonata op. 31. II; in the Marcia Funebre from op. 26 it almost suggests a two-bar question and a two-bar answer; in op. 31 the contrast of the metre, 2 + 2, is very striking. The relative section should always form a contrast with its antecedent section, the contrast becomes even more prominent if the antecedent section ends with a half close on the dominant, the relative section with a full close on the tonic. For example:

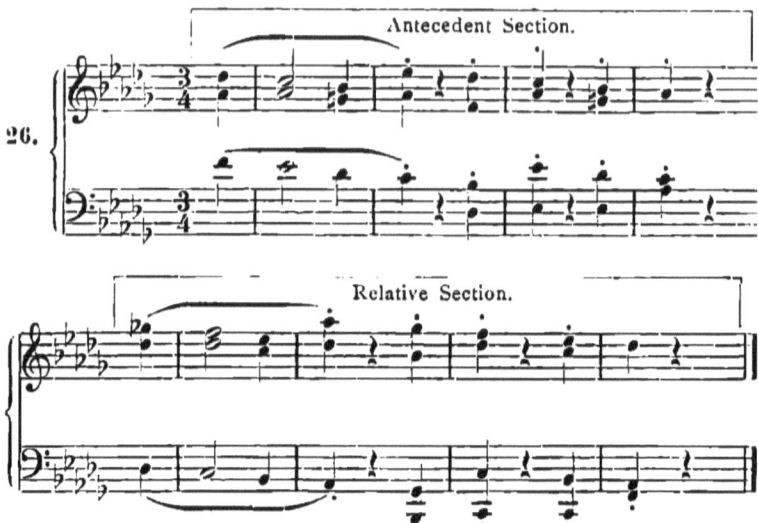

The case may however be inverted, so that the antecedent section of the period contains the full close, the relative section the half close; as in the next example.

In this case the period is not final and does not bring the melody to a termination. Still eight-bar melodies are found to be an exception rather than a rule. Where they do occur, they require a continuation or a repetition. Occurring as an independent piece, as in short songs and choruses, an eight-bar melody demands a double repetition, in order to make an effective whole. The unpleasantness of such small pieces is toned down if they are attached to another strain. Weber proceeds in this manner with the eight-bar gipsy's chorus in Preciosa. After the melody has been sung to three verses, Weber employs eight bars of the gipsy's march, adding to this four bars of coda in order to make a satisfactory close upon the fifth bar.

In order to make a perfect melody two eight-bar periods at least are generally necessary; and in these we frequently find the relative section of the second period repeating that of the first. The Volkslied, already quoted in Ex. 25, gives us an example.

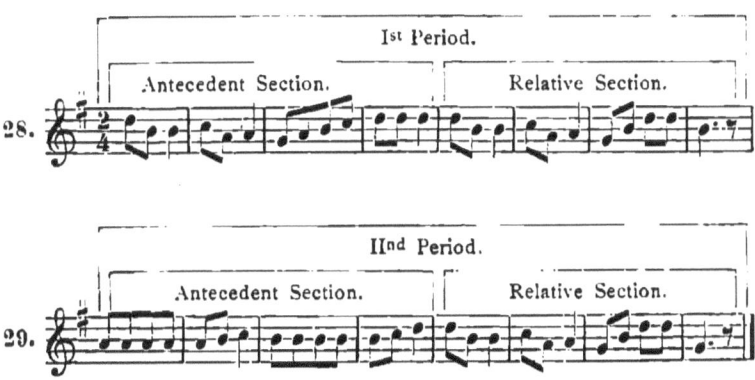

Mendelssohn in his beautiful song "O Thäler weit," similarly repeats the relative section of the first period in the second; with this difference, that he has added five bars to lengthen the close. In spite of this familiar use, the second period is usually employed to form a contrast to the first. This appears still more striking if the second period contains a different relative section from the first; and this is also the case when the second period is developed from the motive of the subject.

14 The Development of Melody.

In this instance the rhythm of the motive is firmly retained in each individual bar of the two periods; a striking contrast results from the alteration of the melodic plan of this motive as well as from the harmonic changes of the accompaniment which naturally ensue. The previous examples 28, 29 and 30 distinctly show that the relative section of each period forms a contrast to the antecedent section, as well as one period does to the other.

That this contrast may be in force when both contrasted sections end with a similar cadence, is proved in the minuet to Beethoven's Sonata op. 49. II, where both sections end on the tonic; or further in the second movement of Sonata op. 10. II, in the Andante of op. 14. II, in the first movement of op. 26, in the trio and minuet of op. 31. III; in all these cases both sections end with a close on dominant. The contrast may arise from an interchange of dominant and tonic cadences or vice versa, as in Ex. 30. Additional examples may be found in the following of Beethoven's works.

Minuet and Trio op. 10. III.
Third movement, second subject op. 10. I.
First movement, first subject op. 10. I.
Rondo op. 13.
Rondo op. 49. I.
Second movement op. 31. I.

All these are instances of the first section terminating on the dominant; examples of the contrary will be found in the Rondo op. 22 and the Scherzo op. 28. We find a half close at the end of the first four bars and a full close at the termination of the next four in the Rondo of op. 22.

Another cadential contrast occurs when the antecedent section terminates in a minor key, the relative section in a major one; this can be observed in the Marcia Funebre op. 26. A similar effect can be found in the first movement of op. 49. I, where the first four bars terminate on the subdominant, the subsequent eight on the dominant.

A contrast may be effected by the entrance of the relative section in a major key, as in the Andante op. 28, or vice versa as in the Adagio op. 53.

An effective contrast may also be made by means of transposing a phrase into a distant key, or by placing it higher as in the first movement of op. 57, or lower as in op. 53. Sometimes the contrast arises from the arrangement of the metre itself as in the Marcia Funebre, where it has the effect of a question and an answer. Similar contrasts may be also found in the second subject of the Finale of op. 10. I, and in the second movement of op. 31. I.

Formation of Melody by Combination of Periods.

§ 3. We have so far shown the pupil how a period is developed from a motive, and a melody from two periods*).

---

* The melody from Preciosa, already alluded to, consists of eight bars, formed from a conjunction of two four-bar periods. The pupils can learn by a reference to the works of the best masters that there can just as well be three, four, five, six or seven-bar periods. But whatever kind of uneven metre be selected, it must always contain a repetition of the first or second period of the even metre in order to form a correct melody, that is to say a musical idea. We often find a third period of six bars, as an extension of the idea, after which four-bar periods enter for the first time. A six-bar period may consist of a combination of two three-bar, or three two-bar metre. A specimen of the latter can be found in the first subject of Beethoven's Concerto in E flat,

Formation of Melody by Combination of Periods.

We can only refer to this; melodies which do not spring from a motive, as in Ex. 3., are simply inspirations of genius. We must leave it an open question whether these sorts of

which is followed by two four-bar periods. In this case the first as well as the second six-bar period consist of a repetition of the first two-bar metre, this is however by no means necessary to the formation of a six-bar period.

18   The Development of Melody.

melodies only arise spontaneously in the imagination of the composer, or whether perfectly refined taste and most highly developed artistic capacity come to the assistance of the author's faculty of creation; in the case of a great genius probably both unite in the construction of Melody. In having received such a number of Beethoven's sketch-books, we have been permitted to obtain a glance into the intellectual

We see in the following Example Serenade by Dr. Jadassohn, op.46, two six-bar periods, each of which is formed from three two-bar metres. The first two-bar metre however does not repeat; hence the first period is immediately repeated but with a new cadence;

workshop of this exalted master. We see from his sketches how often he altered a subject, re-formed it, and frequently changed it from its first insignificant form entirely, leaving it finally as it is employed in the movement of the composition. We shall never be able to know whether in these cases the ideal of his melody at first floated indistinctly in the master's

the continuation consists of four-bar periods.

Seven-bar periods would arise if the close of a four-bar metre is simultaneous with the commencement of a second four-bar metre, in the fourth bar of the period, as shown in the following example from Dr. Jadassohn's third Symphony, op. 50.

mind's eye; or whether it was at first conceived by degrees, and then became distinctly recognisable; or whether Beethoven

The five-bar period is similarly fashioned, still it can also be formed by the combination of a three-bar and a two-bar metre. The two subsequent five-bar periods are taken from a Concerto by Spohr.

31 d.

Just in the same manner the seven-bar period can consist of the combination of a three-bar and a four-bar period or vice-versa. We have purposely avoided mentioning other than four and eight bar periods in the text, lest we should confuse the pupil and suggest the employment of the rarer and more extraordinary forms in his first attempts at composition. These short additional remarks may serve later as an explanation of the more unusual period-formations.

not content with the first fruits of his inspiration, worked and laboured at the subject until he — pardon the simile — had freed and purified the gold of his melody, conceived in the depths of his soul, from all dross. The perfect artistic individuality of his rich fantasy had no doubt assisted him in this case. This will be more apparent as a decided principle presents itself in so many of Beethoven's subjects, no matter whether they be formed from a motive or otherwise. If we regard the subject in Ex. 3, we observe that its highest note only occurs once, as if it were the culminating point of the melody. The same principle is to be found in the subject of the Funeral March in the Eroica, in the subject of the variations in the Kreutzer Sonata, and in many other subjects by Beethoven. This highest note, this melodic acme of the subject frequently appears first at the close of a period, or even of the subject itself. In the works of Schubert and other classical composers we find the same principle at work. We possess however no sketch-books from the other masters, and do not believe that they, though working on the same lines, have so carefully sketched out their mentally developed ideas, as Beethoven has done. Perhaps his deafness obtaining the upper hand, and the impossibility of deciding by ear what floated through his mind, compelled him to write down all his inspirations and their transformations; or perhaps he jotted down his ideas merely to assist his memory. It is certain that other composers have often and substantially altered their first inspirations even if they have not committed them all to paper. Little as we consider ourselves capable of being able to lay down a principle for the formation of a beautiful and graceful melody, or indeed of giving a system for it, still we must offer to the pupil for his first efforts at composition all in our power, in fact everything that has struck us as noteworthy and characteristic in our studies of the classical scores.

A book of this nature should always suggest problems to the student, and should as far as is possible, provide such means as will make their solution easy for him, show him how he can, according to his talent and capacity, obtain a surer footing and greater freedom in his command and control of them. Let the purely mechanical method which we recommend for the beginner's use, be judged from this stand-point; if the more-gifted pupil should not require this aid in forming his periods and sections, still it would surely render him good service in rousing and stimulating his faculties, even if he only regards it as an ingenious invention, serving as a study previous to his handling the Variation-form.

The pupil should now invent a succession of notes, the simplest possible, arranged in an eight-bar period, as shown below.

Let him next endeavour to clothe this stiff strain with rhythmical life, at the same time he may connect the sustained notes by inserting others between them, thus investing the original dry frame-work with a more melodious character, as shown in Ex. 32.

The pupil may, even by this easy and simple study, show and develope his taste, delicacy and artistic insight; and he might vary it in a manner different to Ex. 32, by employing other groupings, until he was enabled to obtain a naturally sequent, harmoniously melodic succession, which, as an eight-bar period, now requires the necessary continuation of a further period of eight bars. Because it follows as a natural consequence, this further period will prove easy of construction. Our next example is a continuation of our last.

Formation of the Close of a Melody.

§ 4. This second period gives cause for some remarks. It contains nine instead of eight bars; this is by no means a disproportion, for the ninth bar is indispensably necessary for the close of the strain. The pupil should take to heart the fundamental rule: **A perfect close must in every instance fall upon the first part of a rhythm and a metre** [*].

When the pupil has modelled a melody upon this plan, let him surround it with a harmony at once natural, healthy and not far fetched; as Ex. 34 shows.

---

[*] A few isolated exceptions to this rule may be found in the works of Mozart and Beethoven. For instance in the airs to the variations in Beethoven's Sonatas op. 109 and op. 111, the second eight-bar period ends on a weak beat. The Adagio of his Sonata op. 31. II, ends upon the last, sixth and weakest beat of the bar: thus —

This forms the close of three two-bar metres, of which the first two have their cadence upon the first beat of the third bar. Had the third metre closed in like manner, it would have necessitated the addition of a bar.

At this stage we must earnestly warn the student against endeavouring to be always "interesting and original" in his first

Let no one imagine for a moment that we are suggesting the insertion of a bar. The evident irregularity of this gently fading cadence is the less apparent to the audience because the performer would surely prolong it, even if ever so little, by a ritardando; thus giving the idea that the final note is the first of another bar.

It would be more difficult to give an explanation of a close on the third beat in common time, such as are occasionally found in Mozart's works. Such exceptions usually occur so seldom that they do not call in question the rule which we have given. In this, as in all other questions of art, a natural taste for what is correct, beautiful and symmetrical should alone decide.

attempts, or against overloading a simple melody with harmonic extravagances. Let him however not worry if his attempts bear resemblance to other known works. The student must first learn to work from a model before he can write with freedom and independence. Further, he must strive to adjust his mind for the conception of what is natural, beautiful and symmetrical. The greatest genius himself imitated, perhaps unawares, the works of his precursors, before he was enabled to develope a style of his own. The youthful efforts of all masters, be they well or little known, bear a striking and speaking testimony upon this point. Let any one study the juvenile works of Beethoven and they will be surprised to see from what small, insignificant and unlikely beginnings this master-mind had developed. The same holds good of the other well-known masters. Unassuming as the intellectual value, nay, the musical ideas themselves may be in the earlier efforts of the masters, one factor stands prominently forward, and that is the idea of order, symmetry, musical architecture, the development of a whole, the natural context of the individual parts, the structure of a composition, in short everything that we understand by the term, Musical Form. In the following chapters, we will endeavour to lay this clearly before the student.

CHAPTER II.

SONG AND SIMPLE SONG-FORM.

The melody of a song.

§ 5. The easiest as well as one of the most interesting studies for the pupil is the composition of songs. The initiate has in this case a frame-work for the structure of his melody both in the rhythm and metre of the text; at the same time he has an opportunity to develope his powers of melody. The prevailing themes of the verse act as a favourable stimulant upon his musical fecundity; on the other hand the narrow range of the human voice compared with that of other instruments, the piano for instance, compels him not to overstep certain limits for the vocal melody. At the same time care must be taken that the melody is good and easy of execution. A diatonic melody is more suitable for singing purposes than a chromatic passage or a mere succession of the notes of chords. We see from the instrumental works of the classic masters what a very important part diatonic melodies play. In proof of this we suggest the two following from Beethoven's Quartett op. 59.

The first of these two only contains the diatonic notes of F minor, in fact a range of seven notes; the second is a diatonic combination of the notes of the scale of A minor. What an extraordinarily marvellous effect, what an inexplicable magic they exercise over us, is known to everyone. We could produce longer themes of this sort whose beauty is equally great; take for example the second subject of the first movement of Chopin's Concerto in E minor. This contains within eight bars only diatonic notes of the scale of E major, excepting two intervals of a minor third. These indications may suffice for the structure of a melody. Naturally it is not intended that only scale-passages are to be employed. We would emphatically warn the pupil against the employment of intervals difficult of execution, whether chromatic or formed from the notes of a chord, as ill adapted for the purposes of song.

For the benefit of making divisions of melody clearer to the pupil we would cite as instances of melodies formed on scale passages the Volkslieder "Liebchen Ade" and "Long, long ago"; as melodies founded on the notes of chords, "Tyroler sind lustig", "Hoch vom Dachstein an", "Uf en Bergli", "Wann i an der Früh"; as a sample of Instrumental melody, the following.

The best proof of the suitability of a melody for vocal use, is to sing it or to allow it to be sung, without the aid of an accompaniment.

Songs in which each Verse is set to the same Music.

§ 6. The next problem for the student is to compose songs in which each verse is repeated to the same melody. The youthful artist will soon observe, if he looks over the songs of Beethoven, Mozart, Schubert, Weber, Mendelssohn, Schumann and other masters how many compositions of extraordinary beauty already exist in this narrow, limited frame-work. We will only mention Mendelssohn's wellknown song, "Leise zieht durch mein Gemüth". We would further recommend for the selection of text, verses for children and national lyrics. The accompaniment requires to be as simple as possible; the compass should not extend beyond ten or eleven notes. The touching melody of the Russian air "Scht ihr drei Rosse" is limited to a minor tenth; whilst the compass of "Schöne Minka" does not exceed a minor seventh. Melodies which do not overstep an octave or a ninth are constantly to be met with. The opening strain of Schubert's Symphony in C proves that a great and noble musical thought can be expressed within the smallest range; this melody which entrances us with its secret and mystical magic, all lies within a minor seventh. The theme from Beethoven already quoted in Ex. 35, has throughout its range, not an extensive compass.

38.

In order to give some variety to his work the pupil can, after he has written a number of solo-songs with piano accompaniment, compose some duets and afterwards some trios for female and children's voices, always working on the same model; passing later to four-part songs for mixed voices, to come at last to four-part songs for male voices. We would recommend as a pattern for the latter, Mendelssohn's lovely four-part song "O Forest deep and gloomy"; at the same time however advising a searching inquiry into all the good music of the kind. The pupil should learn to know the best works of all the different composers, for only by this means can he guard against imitating or copying the style of one author in particular, whether intentionally or otherwise. So would the young artist best avoid falling into the "mannerisms" of his favorite author. Any peculiarity of a work is hardly ever made clear by studying the compositions of one author only; this is generally gained only by a deep research into the works of all.

This warning appears to us so much the more necessary at the commencement of this manual and in beginning composition, since so many youthful aspirants persist in having a "favorite author" on whose pattern they would alone mould their style. This is not difficult to account for: the pupil is positively taken possession of by the works of 'his' master; this composer overpowers him in such a manner that he finds no attractions in the works of any other, in fact an indifference, indeed under certain circumstances, a positive abhorrence of them. In this respect every man is the child of his epoch, and the younger ones are this in a greater degree than their elders. Our students of to-day are often attracted and impressed by the important composers of the present to such a degree that they exhibit a certain distaste against those authors who belong nearer to the dawn of musical history. That the studies then become one-sided, that the prominent works of celebrated masters are neglected because "they are too dry", these are common facts, occurring every day, which any practical teacher will confirm. The pupil should however be brought up to a knowledge of the beautiful in Art. That which makes the most impression for the moment is not always the noblest and most beautiful; even were this the case, the student must learn to know the Good and Beautiful of all composers and all epochs, if he himself wishes to soar to the heights of his art.

For the better comprehension of this form of composition we add a list which we would advise the pupil to refer to.

a. Simple Song-Form, consisting of one period and two sections.

1. Bald grass ich am Neckar.
2. Kommt a Vogerl geflogen.
3. Seht ihr drei Rosse (perfect eight-bar period and repetition of last section).
4. Die Sonn' erwacht (Preciosa).
5. Wo a klein's Hüttl steht.
6. Leise zieht durch mein Gemüth.
7. Es ist bestimmt (two five-bar periods).

b. Simple Song-Form of two periods, the second containing a repetition of the first.

1. Steh nur auf, steh nur auf (a four and eight-bar period, the eight contain the first four).
2. Muss i denn, muss i denn (ditto).
3. Und schau ich hin ($8 + 16$ the latter contains the former).
4. God save the Queen (one six-bar, one eight-bar period).

c. Simple Song-Form with three periods.

Haydn's Hymn to the Emperor.

d. Combination of three and four periods.

Der rothe Sarafan.

e. Five Periods.

Wer hat dich, du schöner Wald.

Simple Song-Form in Instrumental Music.

§ 7. Before we introduce the pupil to the protracted song-form, in which each verse requires distinct and characteristic music, as in the Ballad, the Aria or the Cavatina, let us show how the simple song-form is employed in instrumental works. The simple song-form is most usually found in slow movements, in the air with variations, also in rondos, minuets and final movements. It is moreover also employed in the first movements of some of the greater works, but only under certain conditions. For instance, when a slow introduction precedes the first movement, strictly so-called; or when the first movement begins with a moderate tempo, as for example in the first Allegro in Mendelssohn's A minor Symphony; or again, if the first movement be slow, as is the case in Beethoven's Sonata in C sharp minor.

We divide simple song-form into four different kinds; the *first* of these only occupies one eight-bar period. We give as an example, the beginning of the Adagio from Beethoven's Sonata in B flat, op. 22.

The four cadential bars following this eight-bar period form a codetta, added to the main idea for the purpose of making a close. The main idea itself is clearly expressed in the first period. As another example of the first kind of simple song-form we insert "Die Sonn' erwacht" from Weber's Preciosa.

Necessary repetition in pieces of short duration is well exemplified in Mendelssohn's Gruss; we submit this example, frequently referred to as "Leise zieht durch mein Gemüth".

41.

As an example of two five-bar periods, we give Mendelssohn's "Es ist bestimmt in Gottes Rath".

42.

Beethoven's Adagio in op. 7 contains an eight-bar period with a repetition; in his Sonata op. 49. II, the Tempo di Minuetto has a four-bar period with a repetition. The development of this shortest song-form will no doubt prove a somewhat difficult task for the pupil, because it requires so manipulating that a complete musical idea is clearly represented within the scanty frame-work of an eight-bar period. Since however the study is very instructive, particularly in arousing and exercising his powers of invention, we cannot forego the tasks relative to it.

The *second kind* of simple song-form consists of an eight-bar period which is repeated with a varied cadence. The first period in a major key generally terminates with a half close, but sometimes with a full close on the dominant; in a minor key the first period may end with a cadence on the dominant or in the relative major. The second period always terminates in the key of the piece. We give an example taken from the commencement of the Allegretto in Beethoven's Sonata in E minor op. 14. I. The first period ends in this case with a half close on the dominant; the repetition of this period effects a return to the principal key by means of a full close.

The pupil will find another striking example of this kind in a major key by referring to the first sixteen bars of the Adagio in Beethoven's Sonata in C minor, op. 10. I. We would also refer to op. 7, in which the Rondo contains a four-bar period repeated; the same occurs in the Rondo of op. 31, and in the Scherzo of op. 31. III, as well as in the air with variations, op. 26, where the eight-bar period is repeated.

The *third* kind of simple song-form is that formed by means of two distinct periods. The second period must always form a contrast to the first, even if it repeats a metre from the first. The first period can close at discretion, either upon the tonic, dominant or by means of an interrupted cadence upon a related key; the second period must close upon the tonic only. By way of example we submit the first portion of the Andante from Beethoven's Sonata in G, op. 14. II.

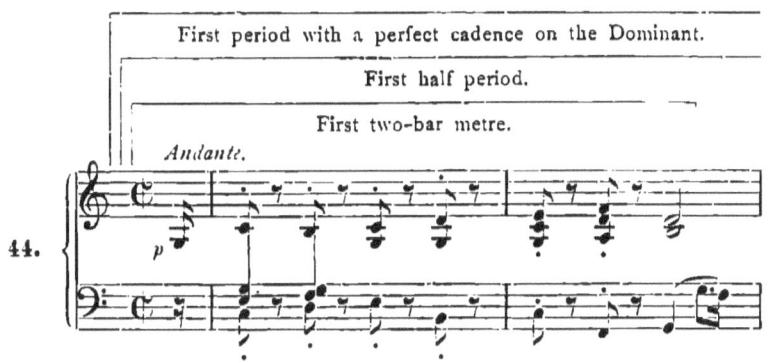
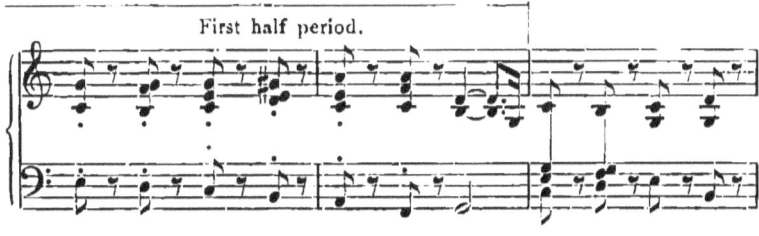
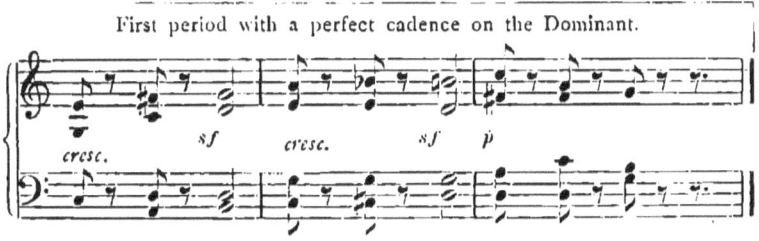

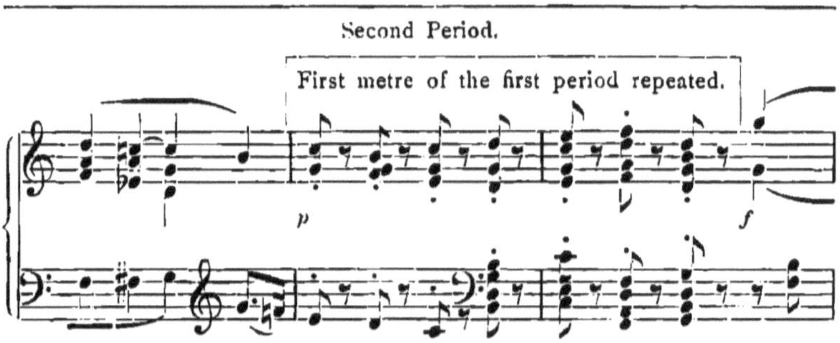

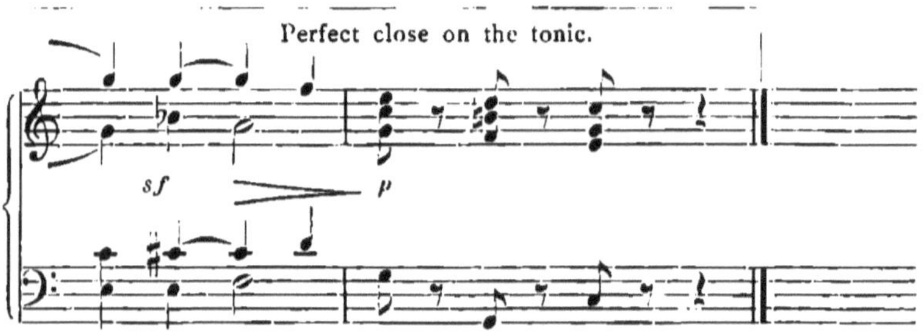

Another good example can be found in the Andante of Beethoven's Sonata op. 57; in this case the first period ends in the principal key, D flat major. For further examples we would refer the student to the Largo of Beethoven's Sonata op. 10. III; here we find two four-bar periods, the first of which closes on the subdominant; the Minuet of the same work contains two eight-bar periods, the first concluding with a half close on the dominant; and also to the airs with variations in op. 109 and op. 111.

Simple Song-Form in Instrumental Music.   37

The *fourth kind* of simple song-form presents itself as a combination of three or four periods, of which the last consists of a repetition of the first, with a full close in the tonic. If we turn to the Adagio of Beethoven's Sonata Pathétique we find the principal idea is given out in the first eight-bar period. This period is repeated exactly but an octave higher, and with a richer accompaniment. A six-bar period follows, which commencing in the relative minor, leads through the principal key (A flat) to the dominant (E flat). A second period of six bars, leading back to the principal key, is attended by an exact repetition of the first eight-bar period. We subjoin a short example of four four-bar periods, taken from Beethoven's Sonata in G, op. 49. I. The first period closes in the fourth bar with a half close on the dominant and repeats in order to terminate with a full close on the tonic. A period of four bars with a half close on the first inversion of the dominant seventh follows as a means of connection, and then comes the repetition of the second period with a full close in the principal key. This is perhaps the shortest example of simple song-form, composed of three connected parts, which can be found.

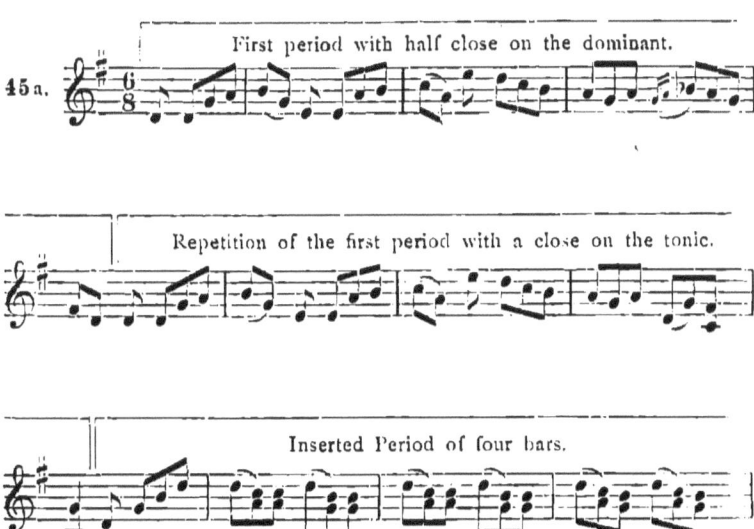

15 a. First period with half close on the dominant.

Repetition of the first period with a close on the tonic.

Inserted Period of four bars.

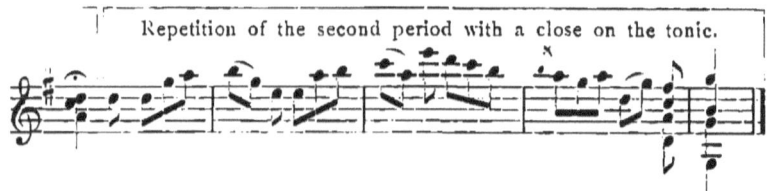

This fourth kind of simple song-form presents manifold varieties, as the pupil can observe in the works of the best masters. We will only hint at some of them at present. For example we find in the Andante of Beethoven's Sonata op. 28, a first period of eight bars, which closes in the minor mode of the dominant. The subsequent period of eight bars, forming a middle portion, is occupied uninterruptedly upon the dominant seventh of the prevailing key. To this is added a third and new period, commencing with and developed from the motive of the first; this comes to a conclusion in the principal key, and the whole constitutes an example of threefold simple song-form. The repetition of the second and third periods will be found in Ex 45 b.

Simple Song-Form in Instrumental Music. 39

The second movement of Beethoven's Sonata in E minor, op. 90, commences with a four-bar period, which is immediately repeated an octave higher. Both periods close in the tonic. These two periods which together occupy eight bars, give place to a second eight-bar period, which beginning in the key of the dominant, likewise closes in the tonic. These eight-bar periods are repeated, and followed by a repetition of the first period of four bars, and this, with a slight alteration, also ends in the tonic. We have in this instance six full closes in the original key within thirty two bars; this, as it stands, is a case rarely to be met with.

The pupil may now collect from the classical works as many instances of the simple song-forms as possible, and afterwards make some attempts to write examples of these four species. It would repay him best to compose something new and varied at each effort, not relying upon his previous work for his ideas. The more he exercises his imaginative faculties, the more they will prove capable of doing. In order to stimulate the power of imagination and not to fall into beaten tracks, let him change the key and tempo of his short movements more frequently. He should seek to give a different character to each piece, so that each requires a new tempo. The pupil should imagine that he has now to compose the commencement of a serious Adagio in duple time, now that of bright rondo or minuet in triple time, and thus test his own powers in every imaginable way. This is without a doubt more difficult than to help one's self out with melodies already employed; besides it is more interesting, praiseworthy and useful to seek and develope new material for every fresh trial.

We shall have occasion later to speak of protracted songform, in which the twofold and threefold combinations receive the addition of a lengthened coda, such as we find in many Adagios; for instance in the Adagio of Beethoven's Sonata in C minor, op. 10. I, again in the Largo of his Sonata in D major, op. 10. III, also in the Adagios of op. 26, op. 31. III, op. 31. II; at this point it would be too early, and would break into our practical course, besides interrupting the exercises and work of the student.

CHAPTER III.

VARIATION-FORM.

The different Kinds of Variations.

Just as the works of the classical masters are the manifestations to us of the innermost workings of Art, so are their studies and preparations a precedent to us which we ourselves should study, and which we should present to our pupils in order that they may reach their destined goal. Amongst the youthful efforts of that great and noblest of tone-poets, Beethoven, is to be found an immense number of variations, some on airs of his own composition, some on those of others; and in the astonishing series of immortal works by this composer, we find the variation-form constantly occurring in every imaginable class of work. Granted that all the other classical masters, Bach, Händel, Haydn, Mozart. Schubert, Weber, Mendelssohn, Schumann and others have written numerous and charming movements in variation-form, still none of them have employed this form with such peculiar charm as Beethoven himself. Variations have a place in every possible description of instrumental composition from his pen; even in the wide field of Symphony, he did not despise its employment. This is sufficient proof for the fact that this form is capable of taking as high a place as any, despite the fact that it had almost run to ruin, owing to the superficial work produced in an age not long past. This shallow ware which was partly intended for teaching purposes, in part also as a means to show the technique of the performer upon 'his' instrument, we can hardly call an art-form, any more than we could call certain fashionable pieces, which hardly deserve the title of Potpourri, Fantasias. The Fantasias of Bach, Mozart, Beethoven, Mendelssohn and Schumann show us what we ought really to understand by this title.

Mendelssohn and Schumann were the first to reinstate the variation-form; the former by his Variations Sérieuses, the most beautiful and important of this gifted composer's pianoforte works, the latter by his lovely variations for two pianos. Although both composers have written other movements in this form, still we have just selected these two prominent works, because we considered them generally best known.

The means for constructing variations are manifold; of the many we would mention the alteration of the motive contained in the air, étude-variations upon a motive, the repetition of the subject with melodic adornments as employed by Bach, the alteration of both motive and subject as in the 'working out' of a symphony or sonata. Further developments may be obtained by an alteration of the motion yet retaining the rhythm, by a change of both harmony and rhythm, by a change of key and by the employment of the major and minor modes.

If we introduce to the more lengthy composition of variations the pupil so soon after his first efforts, we do so on the following grounds. The pupil must now employ a subject in every one of its possible changes; by so doing he has to a certain extent prepared the way for the free fantasia or 'working out'; he must out of one and the same subject gain a number of new forms which are merely developments of it. As in one variation he is still held within the boundary of a form, narrow but easy to survey, so the number of combined variations always appears to him as an extended whole. The individual variations must not of course be placed next to one another spontaneously, but must follow naturally, thus constituting an artistic entirety. How this should be done we will endeavour to lay clearly before the pupil with the help of the "classics". We would first call attention to the fact that we distinguish between two different kinds of variations: viz.

1. Those in which the melody of the subject being but very slightly altered by means of the rhythm, remain easily recognisable throughout all their variations, in which case the harmony for the most part also remains the same.
2. Those in which the melody of the subject furnish the material for new melodic developments, which are formed so unlike the subject, that it is hardly possible to recognise the theme in the variations except as the primary germ of what it has itself produced.

Let us proceed to study the former kind which is easier to construct. As a brilliant example that even in this form the most noble works may be constructed, we would suggest the variations from Beethoven's Sonata Appasionata, op. 57. Before we pass to this, let us say a few words concerning the subject most suitable for variations.

The Subject.

§ 9. Beethoven has proved in his charming and wonderful variations in C minor, that it is possible to construct a splendid movement in this form upon a subject of only eight bars duration. As a rule however subjects made up of two eight-bar periods would be more suitable. At times we find subjects with even three periods in which case the third period is a reproduction of the first, as for example in the first movement of Beethoven's Sonata op. 26. Longer melodies prove themselves less suited to the strict variation-form. The subject should be short and easily intelligible and should contain a clear and distinct musical idea.

The shortness of the melody requires in most cases a repetition of the periods which form the divisions of the subject. By this means the melody is more readily grasped and more easily recognised when it appears in the different variations. Beethoven treats the subjects of the variations in op. 57, 109 and 111 and many others, as a melody of two periods of eight bars each, each of which forms a distinct portion of the subject, and the repetition of each portion is written out in full. If we give our attention to the above mentioned Sonata, op. 57, we shall see a melody, magnificent, sublime and pathetic, which is composed of only a few notes, and whose range does not exceed an octave. In a melodic, harmonic and rhythmic respect, the second period presents a decided contrast to the first; only the final bars of both periods are similar. The melody is so little altered in the variations that it remains distinctly recognisable throughout. The variations consist only of an alteration of the accompaniment; and the harmony continues for the most part the same.

The first variation presents a melody and harmony in staccato notes of equal value, sometimes quavers, sometimes semiquavers, whilst the bass by means of syncopation follows with sustained quavers. The second variation produces a passage in semiquavers, where the melody is distinctly perceptible above the broken chords. We represent this in the following manner.

The motion of this variation is doubly accelerated as compared with the first. To this another double acceleration occurs where the subject is accompanied by demisemiquavers, altered for the most part by syncopation, but the notes of the melody are faithfully reproduced in the first period. At the repetition of the first period we come across the melody both in the syncopated notes of the left hand as well as in the demisemiquaver figure of the right in the first and second bar; in the fourth quaver of the second bar however they only appear above the demisemiquavers. This is shown below.

45 d.

Beethoven makes the entrance of the melody stand out prominently by means of the sforzando. The connection of the first repetition is readily recognised as taken from the figure in the bass.

At the close of the third variation Beethoven produces the subject in sustained notes just as at first, only the bass is altered in the third and fourth bars to demisemiquavers, which still allow the notes of the melody to be easily recognised.

A similar treatment occurs in the seventh and eighth bars, but the period does not repeat. To this is attached in an almost unaltered shape, the second period which does not terminate, but forms by means of a diminished seventh a connecting link with the Finale.

The return to the subject in its originally placid motion after the various accelerations it has undergone, or at least a return to a calmer motion than in the last variation occurs repeatedly, and in every instance with a good effect. We can here only call to mind the variations in Beethoven's B flat major Trio, op. 97, where the subject, with some harmonic alterations is reproduced in tempo primo, and the movement is brought to a close in a steady time in the gentle motion of quavers in triplets. Many similar instances will at once occur to a connoisseur of musical literature, and it is therefore unnecessary to quote further examples.

The pupil's exercises should now consist of composing a number of variations upon a *given* melody, the alterations to be formed by varying the rhythm and motion and in no wise to be made so striking or so difficult as to hide the subject. We consider it better at the present stage to give the pupil a subject than to allow him to choose or construct one for himself. The pupil would in this way learn how to develope all manner of forms through an alteration of rhythm and motion from apparently unpretending material. This practice should not be regarded as so much wasted time or as a more or less mechanical, spiritless operation; on the contrary, this sort of work should always prove an excellent technical stimulant to composition, so that the talented could here find opportunities to display their tastes, imagination, power of construction and well-cultivated ear. Of course the young student should not regard such work as so many dry school exercises, but should rather take trouble upon every occasion to put forth his best efforts. Volkslieder whose melodies form two periods of eight bars, should be chosen as a subject for variation, such as "Hoch vom Dachstein", "Morgen muss ich fort von hier", etc. The pupil may construct his own subject on these lines later.

More important Variation-forms.

§ 10. The second of the two Kinds of Variations already mentioned, in which other melodic forms are to be developed from the subject, will tax the imaginative faculty of the composer still further. In such variations we frequently find a change of both key and time-signature; and it is usual, if the key be major, to have a variation in the minor mode generally marked "Minore"; should the key however be minor the reverse occurs and it is entitled 'Maggiore'. Towards the termination of a long series of variations a fugue or a fugato-movement may sometimes appear. Mendelssohn in his Variations Sérieuses, has placed a fugato-movement in the middle but this is exceptional. Naturally the subject or even a period of it cannot be employed as a fugue-subject, since the longer and more metrically constituted subjects of this form are not adapted to the construction of the fugue or fugal device. Better for this purpose would be to extract a motive, preferably the first, from the subject and employ this as a fugue-subject. The variations should not end with a fugal device, as the strict polyphonic style is only intended to serve as a change in the variations. The termination should be in the free style in which the subject as well as the whole is conceived. A pleasant change might be introduced amongst a number of variations in the free style, by the employment of canonic imitation.

The Close of the Variations.

§ 11. As we have here to do for the first time with a longer piece, even if it consist of several small movements, we must add a few remarks on the close in general and of the close of a variation-movement in particular. Every piece should terminate in such a manner that its close gives the ear a feeling of perfect completion. It should not break off abruptly, and an insufficient close would make a substantial deduction from the charm of a composition, beautiful in other respects. In Italian music of the present day we find frequent repetitions of the full close, especially where each repetition increases in speed.

49.

This is perhaps a very ordinary but still a very suitable means of giving the feeling of completion. It appears to us from this that the requirement of a perfect close are undeniable. Longer pieces, particularly final movements require a more or less independent coda*).

The termination of the movement the satisfying of the requirements of a perfect close is always the most important object of a coda. If we turn to the Finale of Beethoven's fifth symphony we shall find the ordinary coda accelerating its speed and passing to a presto, so that it shows a certain relationship to the foregoing Italian cadence in its repetition of the full close. In the first sixteen bars of the presto, the harmonies of the tonic and dominant are alone employed. At the twelfth bar from this point we have a half close on the dominant. The first repetition of the four bars forming the half close show an increase of speed, the second repetition accelerates the motion still more. The subsequent twenty-six bars beginning with the initial motive of the subject, contain no other harmonies than those of the tonic and dominant. The last twenty-nine bars of the symphony are made up entirely of the common chord of C, which terminates in the last bar in a unison. The whole of the presto presents nothing more than a single, immense final cadence, which Beethoven found necessary for the monumental structure of his gigantic work.

If we return after this digression to the final movement of variations, we shall always find it longer than any of the preceding ones because it requires the addition of a lengthened close; of course, that is, if the movement is final and does not, as in the Sonata Appasionata, lead to another. The last variation of Beethoven's Trio in B flat major, op. 97, presents

---

*) Concerning the coda of longer movements we shall have to speak by and by, when we come to the Sonata. The completed coda was strictly speaking, first introduced by Beethoven; but we find traces of it both in Haydn and Mozart. Beethoven had by this means provided the keystone for the development of the classial forms, and Codas such as are to be found in the seventh and ninth symphonies and in many other of his works, were never written before.

an example of an enlarged close, although the variation-movement leads directly to the finale. The first movement of Beethoven's Sonata in A flat major, op. 26, contains in the last twenty-six bars a distinct, even if only small coda arising from the last variation. The idea

enters quite fresh, it is neither derived from the subject nor motive, it is attached to the movement only; it is quite a natural idea for a coda, for the purpose of preparing a close and lengthening and bringing the movement to an artistic conclusion.

This is by no means necessary; the pupil should see to it that he does not conclude his last variation as in the foregoing instance, which would undoubtedly require further additions. He may prolong his last variation as seems best suited to him.

This is possible by means of a limited repetition of the chords of a full close with varied rhythm or by richly conceived alterations of a full close, or by the addition of a natural close in the form of a coda. The length of a close can alone be determined by a feeling for what is correct and symmetrical. The pupil will at first err by doing too little, later perhaps by doing too much; by degrees he will clearly grasp the extent and proportion of a close, especially if he studies the closing variations in the classical works, carefully and attentively.

Free Variation-Form.

§ 12. It only remains for us now to call attention to a third and last form of variations, mostly employed by Beethoven. We will only do this *en passant* and return to it in speaking of the slow movement in sonata-form, as work in this form should not be exacted from a beginner. The variations in this species are not separated from one another, but connected by means of intermediary phrases. By way of example we would suggest the slow movement of Beethoven's fifth Symphony and analyse it for the purpose of illustrating the form to the student. The first thing that catches the eye in studying the above-mentioned Andante, is that not only one subject but two are employed in manifold variations. Still a preference is given to the first.

The Andante begins with an eight-bar melody which is accompanied by a bass only. The last two-bar metre, commencing with the third quaver of the sixth bar and concluding with the first quaver of the eighth bar, is then repeated with a fuller harmony so that we have an extended period of ten bars. The second period takes its rise from the third quaver of the tenth bar and repeats its first four-bar metre with a small melodic alteration. The harmony remains in the second metre the same as in the first. The final cadence between the eighth and ninth bars of the second period is repeated twice in following bars, and the subject is brought to a close with the repetition of the A flat major chord in the eleventh and twelfth bar. The second subject also in A flat major commences with the third beat of the twelfth bar. After the previous perfect cadence we can hardly consider this subject as a continuation of the first, although it enters at once in the key of the tonic and commences with a dotted figure, imitative of the initial figure of the first subject. In the eighth bar of this subject Beethoven already introduces the key of the major third, in which he so often has his second subjects. The pupil can refer to the second subjects in the first movements of op. 31 1, op. 53 and other of Beethoven's works. This subject enters with a richer harmony and an accompanying motion of semiquavers in triplets, which at the same time form a kind of variation to the melody. This motion ceases in the fourth bar; then follows that wonderfully effective diminished seventh entering pianissimo the first time, and passing into the key of C major. The second subject now appears amid a glancing fortissimo of trumpets, horns and oboes; the violins and violas varying it with the same movement as the violins alone did before. The subject here shows an adjunct of two bars and sustains the third c—g,

Free Variation-Form.

after which an analagous section enters on the diminished seventh, E, G, B♭ and D♭. This section, considerably lengthened, passes through the chords:

to the dominant seventh of A flat major; and now the first variation of the first ten-bar period of the first subject commences with semiquavers below a sustained clarinet part, which shares the motion in the seventh bar. The second period shows but a slight variation in the semiquavers of the flute solo; otherwise it is given exactly as before. To this follows the second subject with an accelerated motion of demisemiquavers on the violas, which at the same time forms a variation of the subject, and commences once more in A flat major. In the fifth bar of this variation of the second subject, a mysterious effect is produced by the tremulant A on the second violins and violas.

The transition to C major and the continuation of the subject in that key are effected in a manner similar to the first time, only with this difference that the accompanying and at the same time varying motion in the violins and violas adds, if anything, an increased acceleration by means of the demisemiquavers. A corresponding figure to that given in Ex. 53 takes place whilst a modulation to the dominant seventh occurs on the violoncellos. Next follows the second variation of the first eight-bar period without the addition of the two-bar metre; as in the first variation, the violoncellos and violas take up the varying motion. The obligato part given in the first variation to the clarinet is in this instance allotted to the first flute, the oboe and the bassoon. At the eighth bar a further repetition of this variation of the first period commences. The first violins repeat almost note for note the varied figure which the violoncellos and violas had previously. With a slight deviation (probably written for the sake of an easier execution), the violoncellos and doublebasses then take up a second repetition of the variation, which comes to an end upon a half close on the dominant. After the pause a free episode is introduced, for which the initial figure of the first subject, without retaining its dotted rhythm, provides the material. The episode leads to the second subject, which now enters in C major and without other motion than it originally contained. After a short transition the third variation of the first period of the first subject now follows as "Minore" in A flat minor for ten bars; a fourth variation manipulating the first period in free canonic style, succeeds the minor after a short episode, but in major. The second period is added without any variation. From più mosso to the end of the Andante now follows what appears evidently to bear the character of a movement containing two varied subjects. The pupil will meet with other slow movements in this form, for instance the Adagio in the ninth symphony. The foregoing analysis of the Andante of the fifth symphony will no doubt suffice to give a clear insight into this more rarely employed variation-form. The work relative to this form, as has already been remarked, is not yet to be exacted from the pupil.

CHAPTER IV.

DANCE-FORM.

The Contrasted Movement.

Dance-form is developed from the third and fourth varieties of simple song-form. It usually however presents a combination of two different movements in song-form; the second or contrasted of these is called the Trio. *The principal movement must in every case be repeated after the Trio, even should the Trio be written in the same key as the principal movement.* Smaller dance-forms which only yield small pieces of two portions, no matter whether they be formed of two or four periods, can hardly serve for other than the practical purposes of dancing; they would never bring about a satisfactory result owing to their too meagre form. Short dances of only two portions alone produce a piece when several of them in succession form an uninterrupted whole. Thoroughly delightful and charming as the waltzes for four hands by Schubert are, one of these, if played alone, would never give a perfectly satisfactory result; performed successively however, they are heard as a whole. Pieces of two portions constantly occur in the works of the older masters; they are to be found in Sarabands, Gigues and Courantes. But these twofold pieces are then only portions of a Suite. Should such a movement, say a gigue, occur at the close of a suite, each of the two parts requires in most cases to be continued. How strong the necessity for repeating the first movement is, can be seen from the remark at the close of the second of two successive pieces, headed Gavotte I and Gavotte II, that the first must be repeated. It is evident that in this case the second Gavotte forms the trio of the first.

In dance-form all effective pieces are not alone to serve the purposes of the Terpsichorean art, as indeed the Waltz, Tyrolienne, Galop, Minuet etc., are, but are also written as pieces suitable for chamber music and concert music, as the Scherzo, Capriccio and Impromptu. Even the March has no other form than that already explained. If we regard this form closer, we shall observe in most cases that the contrasted movement, the trio, is shorter than the principal one, on rare occasions it may be of an equal length, but never longer. In order to render this form as clear as possible to the pupil, we shall here quote the Minuet from Mozart's Symphony in E flat major. The first part of the principal movement consists of two periods of eight bars each, the first of which is a combination of two four-bar metres, the second of four two-bar metres. This part terminates with a full close on the dominant.

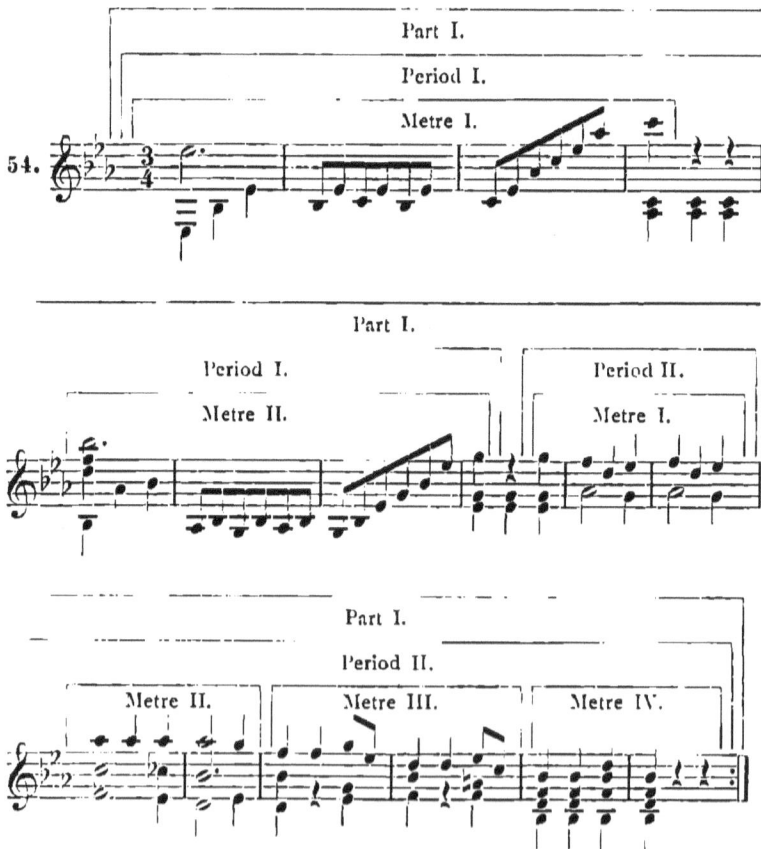

The second portion consists of a period of eight bars, to which however the whole of the first part is added, but with an altered cadence leading back to the key of the tonic. The last period is extended for four bars for the purpose of strengthening the close. Next comes the trio, whose first part consists of a period of eight bars; this has a half close on the dominant at the end of its first four-bar metre, the second metre does not, as usual, close in E flat major,

but, after the repetition of this portion, returns at once to the beginning, and then passes directly to the second portion of the trio, to which it forms a contrast in a melodic, harmonic, rhythmic, and metrical respect. We have for the first six bars nothing but one-bar metres, to which a two-bar metre is added for the sake of completing the period.

The period ends, strictly speaking, upon the first crotchet of the seventh bar; the last two additional bars form a transition to the first portion of the trio, which is now added to complete the second portion of the trio. Each part of the Minuet and Trio is to be repeated, save that in the repetition of the principal movement after the trio, the *reproduction* of the separate portions does not take place.

This Minuet of Mozart's may serve as a pattern of dance-form on small lines. Small as it is, it still remains in itself an independent piece, which by the additional four bars in the second period of the second portion of the principal movement forms a satisfactory conclusion. The reason of the feeling of satisfaction, which we receive from the Minuet lies partly in the fact that the whole piece is written throughout in one key. This occurs also if the principal movement in minor is followed by a trio in the major mode of the same key; as for example in the Minuet of Mozart's Symphony in G minor and in Beethoven's first Sonata, op. 2. I. A similar effect is gained when a Minuet in a major key is followed by a trio in the minor form of the same key, as in the Scherzo of Beethoven's Sonata in A major, op. 2. II. A persistence in the same key belongs to the nature of very small movements. The necessity of forming the trio in another key is not in itself so pressing as it is in the case of more extended movements in protracted forms. Beethoven does not merely retain the trio in the same key in the Minuets and Scherzi written in the more limited forms, such as those mentioned above or in Sonatas op. 27. II or op. 31. III, but he also carries out the same principal in the much broader conceived Scherzo movements of the fourth, fifth and ninth Symphonies, of Sonata op. 7, of the Violin Sonata, op. 30. II, and of the Sonata op. 106. We find the same principle in the other masters, for instance in the Minuet of Mozart's Jupiter Symphony. We do not advance the absolute necessity of changing the key of the trio; it should in every instance be left entirely to the author's fancy, whether he will retain the key of the principal movement, or whether he will permit a change of key for the trio. The pupil find no hard and fast rules laid down here, which will prove absolutely infallible for all cases. With regard to this point we can only show how the masters have proceeded in such cases, i. e., what keys they have employed where a change in the key of the trio does take place. In a major key these will most generally be found to be the relative minor (see Beethoven's Scherzo op. 2. III, Minuet op. 22, and Scherzo op. 28), more rarely the key of the subdominant (Beethoven's Minuet op. 10. III. Scherzo op. 26, Schubert's Scherzo op. 100), and frequently the major key of the submediant (Beethoven's 7th Symphony, Scherzo, Schubert's Symphony in C major, Scherzo). In movements in a minor key we most frequently find the trio in the major mode of the same key, or in the major mode of the minor sixth. As examples of those movements which have their trios in the major mode of the original key we have already cited Mozart's G minor Symphony and Beethoven's C minor Symphony; as instances of those which form their trios in the major key of the minor sixth, we would mention from Beethoven's Sonatas, the Allegretto from op. 10. II, the Allegretto from op. 14. I, and the Allegro molto from op. 27. I.

The pupil can now work a number of small pieces with trios, upon the instructions he has so far received. He would do best to begin with dances such as Waltzes, Tyroliennes, Galops and Polkas and to compose such as might really be employed for dancing purposes. Of course he could then only compose in uniformly regular periods, and would then exercise himself to a certain extent upon a fixed model. This is in any case very useful practice for the beginner who thus learns to confine himself to a strictly limited and small form. The more studies of this sort he makes at first, so much the better will he be enabled to work in broader conceived and freer forms.

But even these small, strictly limited forms allow manifold liberties and present manifold exceptions to Mozart's Minuet, analysed above. It is not always necessary that the trio should have two parts. We find in Beethoven's Sonata op. 28, a two-part trio which really contains one and the same period of four bars repeated six times:

Protracted Dance-Form.   59

These two parts are indeed separated from one another by the double bar, still in the main they form but a single portion, for the musical idea in the two parts is exactly the same. In many dances, marches and characteristic pieces the trio, which according to its nature should ever be smaller than the principal movement, has only one part. On the other hand however we constantly find extensions of the periods, particularly the last period of the second portion of the principal movement, for the purpose of perfecting and emphasising the formation of the close. Even in the midst of a part an inserted period might occur, which would have a modulatory and preparatory character, such as the inserted period of twelve bars in the Scherzo of Beethoven's Sonata, op. 26.

It is difficult to enumerate all the different liberties, which the composer may take even in this small form. Good taste and an intuitive faculty will know how to introduce the correct thing in the right place. Upon a careful study of the movements of this kind in classical works the pupil will discover that all these pieces, even though they differ from one another in some slight measure, are yet formed upon one and the same principle.

Protracted Dance-Form.

§ 14. After the pupil has composed a number of pieces for purposes of dancing, he may write some in dance-form which shall have merely a musical end in view. He will soon find it necessary to deviate from the strict, regular periods of dance-music. Now he must lengthen his last period for the purpose of forming a cadence, as was shown in the extract from Mozart, again he will have to insert a period in the second part by way of preparing an effective entrance of a new period, or of repeating the first portion, as is shown in Ex. 58. This will frequently be the case if the trio closes in a different key from the principal movement. Beethoven introduces the repetition of the principal movement, after the close of the trio, in the Scherzo of the Sonata in A flat major, op. 26, by means of the following four bars:

Such an inserted period can also serve to prepare a new part which has an entirely different rhythm. Beethoven progresses from the trio to the Scherzo in the ninth Symphony through the two following bars:

These two bars contain the motive of the Scherzo four times, in this concentrated form.

Beethoven has also proved in the Minuet of the Sonata op. 31. II, that a coda after the repetition of the principal movement is also necessary in pieces of short duration. In the following case only the rhythmical initial motive is employed to bring about a termination of a plagal cadence on a pedal.

In other cases we find a short independent idea forming the coda. At the close of the Funeral March in op. 26, we come across such a new idea. The March repeats without any alteration after the trio until the final bar, then however Beethoven adds the subsequent bars as coda. These bars contain an idea which is neither found in the march nor in the trio, and which only derives its uneven rhythm on the weak beat from the main idea.

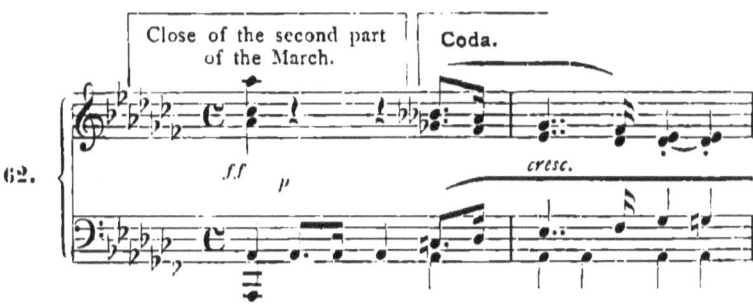

Sometimes a portion of a trio is repeated and employed for the purpose of forming a coda. This occurs in Beethoven's Sonata op. 14. I, in the final bars expressly marked Coda. In this case the commencement of the coda is in a different key to that of the movement. The key of E minor does not enter until the eleventh bar.

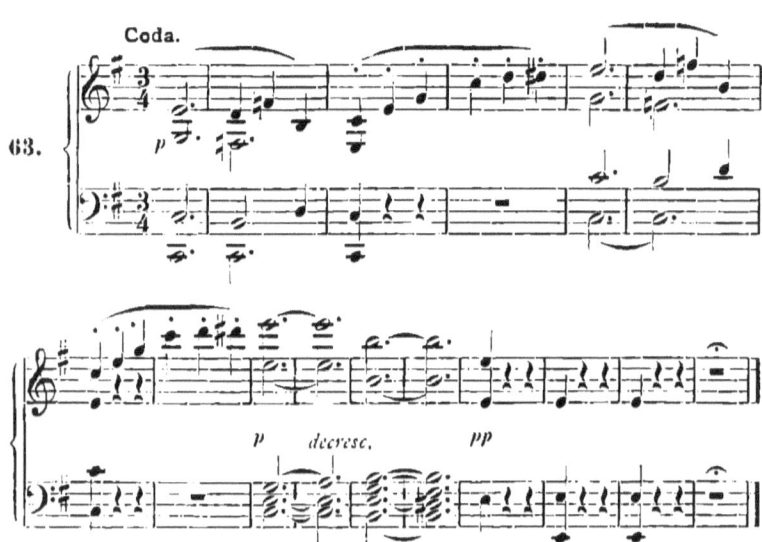

In a similar manner Beethoven employs the main idea of the trio in the Scherzo of the ninth Symphony, where he allows it to appear once more after the repetition of the Scherzo and then concludes the movement with the two bars shown in Ex. 60 to which the final bar is added.

The re-appearance of the trio, as well as the repetition of the trio after the final performance of the principal movement, was first introduced by Beethoven; and we must likewise specify it as a development of musical form, for which we have to thank this great genius. Beethoven thereby emphasises the principle that nothing of importance can appear only once in a movement. In the fourth Symphony, both Scherzo and Trio are repeated after the Trio and finally the Scherzo again. The following idea in the coda concludes the movement:

The case is similar in the Scherzo of the seventh Symphony. Here again after the double repetition of the principal movement, a reminiscence of the Trio is recalled in the coda for the third time by the reappearance of its initial figure:

We occasionally find two separate trios in the later masters, such as Mendelssohn and Schumann. With all due respect for these masters and their works we cannot now discuss this form. For the repetition of both trios would, even if only partially given, have a tendency to be more wearisome than a threefold repetition of the principal movement; and the omission of the repetition of both trios after the second hearing of the principal movement, contradicts the principle that every fresh important idea must occur twice in a movement. This twofold presence of the main ideas compels us then to repeat the individual parts of a work in dance-form; and it is a matter of indifference whether the repetition be represented by the usual signs, or whether it be written out in full, or whether it be exact or slightly varied. We cannot and dare not wilfully omit the repetition of any portion marked "Repeat", without disturbing the form of the whole. Should we omit the repetition of such a portion, we would shorten the whole, and thereby render it imperfect.

The pupil can now proceed with his compositions in danceform; and can gradually venture to extend the individual portions; this cannot happen by lengthening the parts in a mere haphazard fashion. The musical idea must itself rather contain, in a greater or less degree, the condition necessary to further extension. Every musical idea regulates its own form according to its intellectual contents. If this happens then to all musical ideas upon the same principle, it will be difficult to find two pieces of short duration and treated in a free style, somewhat more extended than mere dance-form, which are exactly alike in their plan, structure and in the number of the bars of the whole as well as of the parts. The internal structure of a composition resembles in this point all other organic forms. We never find two leaves in an oak forest exactly alike, nor yet two human-beings perfectly resembling each other, although leaves and human-beings originate and develope upon the same principle. Nature creating on her grandest scales only produces resemblances but hardly ever an exact copy. We are only able to extract from the revelations contained in the works of the masters the principles upon which we must compose, and only from the fact that we feel and recognise the true art in the classical creations are we enabled to assimilate the art forms. This cannot be attained by a slavish reproduction of one or more patterns. Only when the meaning of the organic forms has been awakened and aroused within us, are we able to compose according to our own free fancy and, even then, only after the patterns left by the masters. A jealous research into the classics will in this case alone prove of true advantage. Since for the limited model of strict dance-music we cannot set up a fixed length for its individual parts, nor fixed rules for a regularly recurring order of modulation, or for the length of the principle and contrasted movements, we are far less in a position to be able to give definite exercises for the composition of more extended works constructed on broader lines.

We will not fail at the close of this chapter to draw the attention of the young artist wandering in the labyrinths of counterpoint, that in the second part of the principle movement of the more extended dance-forms he can begin to employ contrapuntal devices. The second portion of the Minuet in Mozart's Jupiter Symphony even in its slight form, as well as in that of his G minor Symphony and in those of many of Haydn's Symphonies and Quartetts, not to mention the works of other masters, already present highly interesting contrapuntal combinations which now and then, (particularly in the Minuet of Mozart's Symphony in G minor), lend the second part the character of a free fantasia in a small degree.

CHAPTER V.

THE PROTRACTED, COMBINED SONG-FORM.

The Song with different music to each verse, the Ballad, the Aria, Arietta, Arioso, Cavatina, Romanza, Scena and Aria, Chorus in Opera and Oratorio.

As there are poems, whose individual verses, at times whose single lines, do not permit from the nature of their contents of being expressed musically in the same way as what precedes or follows, the composer is compelled to clothe the several verses with varied music. Should the meaning expressed in the text, remain for the most part the same throughout the poem, and should another idea only occasionally present itself, it would be as well for the composer to retain the principal melody of the song as far as possible and to repeat it, only deviating where the text permits. Should the poem express a new idea after the first verse, different in its character to that which precedes, the composer must insert a new musical idea such as the text requires.

Much as this new musical idea may differ from what precedes, still it must terminate naturally; the final portion of the composition must also be rendered in the same key as the beginning. We may commence a song in E minor and conclude it in E major, but we can never begin one in F and end it in D or in any other key. To express musically the ideas prevailing in the poem, to adapt the words rhythmically, the lines and verses metrically, to pay constant attention in effecting a joint connection with the sister-art so that the music does not disturb the flow of the verse, this must ever be regarded as the highest aim in the union of lyric poetry and music. Beyond all considerations the unity of the key must be first guaranteed. An exception occurs when a recitative precedes the Aria or song. Such a case is to be found in Schubert's Wanderer where the portion which precedes the words "Ich wandre still" which introduce the melody in E major, are to be regarded as "quasi recitativo". Furthermore the composer must see that the musical form, so far as the text allows of any, is suitable and that it is neatly rounded off by bringing about a repetition of the principal melody. The composer must above all things not lose sight of the fact that in this song-form he has to produce a perfect composition, that this must be invested with a musical form and that this form, so far as is compatible with the idea presented in the text, should approach as nearly as possible that of simple song-form. Should the poem in the course of its progress express two or more entirely different ideas, the composer must then work out so many different movements in song-form, which in their musical connection form a complete whole.

In these protracted songs the accompaniment will play an

important part in illustrating the text. This however should never be carried to such an excess that the accompaniment is brought into undue prominence whilst the voice part is condemned to play a secondary part. How very frequently an accompaniment, completely subordinate to the voice, may have a characteristic effect, can be seen in the songs of the masters. The accompaniment in Schubert's 'Ich hört ein Bächlein rauschen' subordinates itself perfectly to the voice, yet supports and carries it on, still presenting us with a picture of the purling brook, now rushing headlong, now placidly calm. If we turn to this accompaniment which proceeds with an even motion throughout the song,

66.

it presents but a slight difference to the accompaniment of Schubert's "Gretchen am Spinnrade"

67.

which expresses so characteristically, not only the act of spinning but the anxiety and troubled unrest of Gretchen herself. The difference in tempo at the beginning of both songs is by no means so marked that the two parts, though so entirely different are brought into prominence and characterized by a substantial acceleration of the motion in either one or the other. The difference lies in the first place in the major and minor harmonies with which the two songs are clothed; in the second place in their rhythms.

The calm, regular rhythm of the first mentioned song,

presents a decided contrast to the restless throbbing of the second:

even the rhythm of the semiquaver figures in both is quite distinct: for if Schubert does represent the figure

as a sextuplet, in reality it is only a double triplet, as can clearly be seen from the bass.

On the other hand the semiquavers in Gretchen's song present a sixfold figure, divisible thus:

The pupil will observe from a comparison of these two florid accompaniments, how well Schubert, the great song-writer, understood the art of forming a characteristic accompaniment with small means; and this accompaniment far from injuring the voice-part has the effect of supporting and ennobling the song. Both these songs of Schubert are examples of protracted song-form and in both the master has made use of perfectly constituted musical forms, which resemble, so far as the text permits, the style of simple song-form. If we study the first song somewhat closer, the melody of the first eight-bar period expresses to us in the first place, the happy mood of the wandering miller, who, attracted by the purling of the brook, would fain see it.

We can almost believe we hear the hasty elastic step of the youth in the four quavers of the first and fifth bar. He feels a desire to see the stream, at the same time a dim suspicion that the brook may be the cause of an important fatal turning point in his life. The poet remarks this in the words

"Ich weiss nicht, wie mir wurde,
Noch wer den Rath mir gab".

Schubert characterised the feeling of perplexity by means of the hesitating and restless rhythm at the beginning of the second period.

Ich weiss nicht wie mir wur - de, noch   etc.

The interruption which the melody suffers at the commencement of the second beat by the omission of a note has a striking effect, which would certainly never have been attained if Schubert had set the text to the same melody, only with a regular rhythm, as follows:

Ich weiss nicht wie mir wur - de, noch

The last four bars of the second period reproduce the first period with a slight alteration; these four bars are immediately repeated to the same words. The first twenty bars form a first part which closes in the key of the tonic. This is followed by a second part of twelve bars beginning with a modulation to E minor, and this closes in the dominant. An episode of eighteen bars now commences with a deviation to A minor; and it contains the motive of the second part,

hin - un - ter und im - mer wei - ter

which is taken from the motive shown in Ex. 74; the following motive.

und im - mer hel - ler rausch-te

is combined with it to the words "Du hast mit deinem Rauschen mir ganz berauscht den Sinn". The episode leads back to the key of the tonic. Next follows a concise repetition of the melody of the first two parts. The last four bars of the repetition proceed again to the key of the tonic. Schubert allows a repetition of the words "es gehn ja Mühlenräder" to the marvellous melodic flight,

which is a slight variation of the four previous bars. At the words, "Lass singen, Gesell, lass rauschen", he adds a coda.

We have analysed this model of protracted song-form as an illustration for the pupil. The principle of developing a form, grounded upon and similar to the simple song-form, will be found not only in the protracted songs of the masters but also in their arias, ariettas, cavatinas and romanzas.

The ballad is less adapted to compositions in protracted song-form on account of the narrative character of its contents. The composer must construct different tone-pictures in diminutive simple song-form, according to the contents of the several verses; these tone-pictures will not resemble one another and in most cases will not bear repetition. Nevertheless he may be able to fashion a ballad in this form in such a manner that it presents a complete unity. He may employ musical declamation, such as is used in recitative, but that will not alone suffice. How this is to be achieved, depends upon the inventive power and refinement of the composer. In Schubert's Erlkönig the poem commences with a narration; then the speeches of the father, the son and the Erlkönig are introduced. The father begins by questioning and then calming and appeasing his frightened child who is paralysed with fear and cries out with deathly agony; the Erlkönig is introduced with sweet misleading words of love, breaking out at last with an expression of intense passion. The narrative as well as the feelings and susceptibilities of the dramatis personae of Goethe's poem, all lie within the range of a musical composition, which from beginning to end retains the same rhythm and up to the accelerando towards the close, the same tempo, and which terminates in the same key in which it commenced; even its characteristic initial figure

79.

Motive.

is not merely introduced at first, but re-enters in the middle of the song in D minor and again, towards the close, in G minor. Even the number of keys through which the composition moves is somewhat limited. From this the pupil will discover that a change of key, time-signature and tempo is by no means always necessary to express a new idea in music. By a too frequent use of such changes the unity of the piece is destroyed. Compositions of this description easily obtain an appearance of patchiness and scrappiness, in other words a want of musical "Form". Even if the individual portions are really beautiful, and we are pleasantly affected by all the separate portions of a piece, still the composition as a whole may not, on account of its formlessness, exercise, musically speaking, a beneficial and satisfactory effect. In music form and idea are not more inseparably connected that are the soul and body in the human being. A composition without form is as difficult to imagine as a body without a soul. Let the youthful artist make no such mistake, as to seek to arrive at the truth of expression at the cost of the beauty and symmetry of musical form. The arias in Mozart's and Beethoven's operas, in Handel's, Haydn's and Mendelssohn's oratorios, and in Bach's Cantatas, Masses and Passion Music prove that the grandest truth of expression, the very depths of feeling can be described within the limits of strict musical form.

The grand Scena and Aria in operas usually consists of several short simple song-forms strung together. They generally commence with a recitative which is followed by a slow movement, and the whole is brought to a conclusion by a quick movement. This of course depends upon the nature of the text. The several movements may be either separated or connected by short recitatives. As an example of this form well known to all our readers, we would suggest Agatha's Aria in Freischütz, "Wie nahte mir der Schlummer, bevor ich ihn gesehn".

In conclusion we would mention that the more lengthy and extended independent choral-movements in operas which are not composed in simple song-form, are usually designed in the form at present under consideration. The pupil will also find many motets and choruses in the oratorios written in the protracted song-form.

Protracted Song-form in Instrumental-Music.

§ 16. We find the protracted, combined song-form very largely employed in instrumental music. Mendelssohn has written quite a number of beautiful pieces in this form in his Lieder ohne Worte; but long before his time the earlier masters had composed instrumental "Lieder ohne Worte", sometimes with the title "air" or "aria", and sometimes without it. We do not hesitate to describe the fourth, eighth, ninth, tenth, twelfth, twenty-second and others of the preludes from the first volume of Bach's Wohltemperierte Clavier, as such. The twenty-fourth prelude, despite the fact that it is written à 3 voce, seems to us a duet without words, for soprano and alto with a bass accompaniment, even if it has not like Mendelssohn's A flat Lied (op. 38. VI.), the title of "Duet". We will lay clearly before the pupil the protracted song-form employed in instrustrumental music and choose for this, the well-known and beautiful Adagio from the Sonata Pathétique. The first idea, consisting of an eight-bar period (Ex. 3), together with its repetition which is given in full, forms the first part of the principal movement. The next twelve bars form the second portion; this begins in F minor and proceeds to a close upon the dominant in bar 7, and thence makes a return to A flat major. The first part repeats in the next eight bars, and brings the principal movement to a conclusion. Then follows an episode in A flat minor whose initial motive returns in eight bars to E major. This is succeeded by a short modulation back to A flat major. The whole of the first part now repeats, at the same time retaining the triplet motion of the episode in the accompaniment. The last seven bars of the Adagio form a coda to the movement.

We find the mysterious, slow movement of Beethoven's Sonata, op. 10. III, is formed in a similar manner. The principal movement, contracted and with some slight alterations, is repeated after the episode beginning in F major, and this is immediately succeeded by an extended coda. This is taken from the initial motive of the principal movement with an accompaniment of demisemiquavers in sextuplets, but reproduces in its course the passionate demisemiquaver-motive from the episode, which enters upon a six-four chord of the tonic.

80.

A codetta now follows and begins with the final notes of the initial motive.

81.

The form in the Adagio of Beethoven's Sonata in B flat major, op. 22, will be found to be somewhat less extended. This has finally no other coda than that already employed at the close of the principal movement. The following four bars

82.

when transposed to E flat bring the Adagio to a close. Further coda than that employed at the conclusion of the principal movement (Ex. 82), is not required in this instance. Concerning the episode there is nothing further to remark than that it is the motive of the principal movement,

worked out in a contrapuntal style, that is to say, produced in new shapes, but introducing no new idea.

The repetition of the principal movement is very frequently adorned with variations. Sometimes an accelerated motion will be introduced in the accompaniment.

In many cases Beethoven produces several climaxes in the accelerated motion and returning, closes once more with the original placid tempo; at other times he will retain the increase of speed until the very close of the movement. A good example of this can be seen in the Adagio of the Sonata for piano and violin, op. 30.

Beethoven's more extended slow movements, no matter whether they be written in song or variation-form, are distinguished almost throughout by a great multiplicity of motion. The beginner should remember that a lengthy employment of a similar kind of motion has a wearisome effect even in a quick movement, if it be not interrupted in time; this is much more the case in a slow movement. The most beautiful melody with the richest and most interesting harmonic accompaniment would in this case, where an equal motion is retained for a long time, prove wearisome. A long slow movement more than any other requires a frequent change of motion; by this, a change of tempo is not to be understood. To this end let the pupil compare the Adagio of Beethoven's Sonata, op. 30, or that of his fourth Symphony or any other of his Adagios which contain no change of tempo, and he will be astonished at the wealth and variety of the motion in these movements.

So far we have only exhibited the employment of the protracted song-form in slow movements, but we also find it in quick ones when they are not of too great a length. All

Mendelssohn's Lieder ohne Worte in quick tempi are written in song-form and many in their structure resemble the protracted song entirely. It almost seems surprising to us, that so far as we know, no one of the distinguished modern lyric poets has suggested the idea of supplying some of the most beautiful and melodious of these songs with words.

The melody of the "song" in E major, op. 35. III, could, if transposed a third lower, be very easily sung by a soprano; the last five bars of the Lieder are especially adapted to form a conclusion in the accompaniment. Just as in Mendelssohn's Lieder and in Bach's Preludes, we find the protracted song-form also employed in Etudes, Caprices, Fantasias, and in other small instrumental movements both in quick and slow tempi. Cramer's Study in G sharp minor, (vol. II', Moscheles' Study in A minor. (op. 70. V), Chopin's Etude in A flat major (op. 25. I,, Henselt's Etude, La Gondola, many of Schumann's Fantasiestücke, of Field's and Chopin's Nocturnes, should be strictly speaking called Lieder ohne Worte.

The next exercise for the pupil consists in constructing short as well as extended pieces, in the form under consideration, some in slow, some in quick tempo, answering to the models cited above. The compositions should not be merely confined to pianoforte use alone; pieces for piano and violin or violoncello, piano and clarinet, for two violins, for string quartet, for an orchestra of strings only or for a small orchestra, would present a varied field of operation for the beginner. The pupil should remember that it is not good to employ too complicated a machinery for the performance of pieces of no great length, that pieces of very short duration cannot be suitably written for orchestral purpose, unless several consecutive pieces are grouped as a whole. In this case it would be as well to interchange the form of the several small pieces, as can be seen in the suites of the classic masters. In any case the beginner ought first to write a number of small pieces in combined song-form for piano alone, before he proceeds to the composition of extended movements for several instruments or for a complete orchestra.

CHAPTER VI.

RONDO-FORM.

The Rondo without Contrasting Episode.

The Rondo requires frequent repetition of the main idea, interspersed with several episodes. These may either be episodes of contrast, episodes of development, or very often only episodes of transition. Episodes of contrast, such as the Trio in the dance-form repeat partially at least, after the recurrence of the principal subject, or are suggested either by the repetition of the main idea in the Trio or of a characteristic motive of it. It can happen however that the episode of contrast is neither repeated nor in any way even suggested. This is the case in Beethoven's Rondo in the Sonata in C major, op. 53. The special reason for this is to be sought in the development of the melody of this episode of contrast. The subject suggested,

contains a twofold repetition of its initial motive in C minor within its first six bars. The following two bars, which complete the eight-bar period, proceed to A flat major whereupon the whole period is repeated with triplets in semi-quavers in the bass. To this a new period succeeds which is certainly formed from the first; it commences in A flat major and ends in C minor; the triplet passage is then given to the upper part.

Even this period is not only repeated but the last four bars suffer a further repetition. Finally the two last bars repeat twice before the episode of contrast concludes with the following passage.

In this instance the idea of the episode of contrast, formed from a threefold repetition of the motive, repeats frequently, so to speak, within itself, and thereby renders an additional recurrence unnecessary. Upon similar grounds Beethoven does not allow a repetition of the episode of contrast in A flat major, from the Rondo in the Sonata Pathétique:

he does not even permit its recurrence anywhere in employing the motive of the leap in fourths. The five-fold repetition of the main idea in a Rondo is sufficient for his purposes. It is quite evident that the stirring episodes here alluded to, are not merely modulatory, but really independent episodes of contrast, productive of a new idea. No one would assign the character of an episode of contrast to the short modulatory transition beginning in B flat major (in the Rondo of the Sonata in D major, op. 10. III), which however, does not occur again. No one could imagine the following four bars taken from the Rondo of the Sonata in G major op. 31, as an episode of contrast; for despite its difference of character from the main idea, which lends it the stamp of a new independent thought, the motive contained in the subject,  still recurs in a succession of ground basses with a syncopated rhythm;

then the first idea follows immediately and is continued in the next four bars.

The whole double-period is thereupon repeated three times in succession.

The recurrence of the principal subject does not always require to be produced in the key of the tonic; it may also be given at one time unaltered, at another varied. Compare the entrance of the principal subject in A flat major, with an accompaniment of quavers in triplets, in Beethoven's Sonata op. 51. I. The episodes are almost always placed in a different key to that of the principal subject; but it is not good to give them a new time-signature. The tempo, ritardandos and accelerandos excepted, should remain the same throughout the movement; for the form of the Rondo usually so small, loses its completeness, if the time is changed at leisure, or frequently and in a striking manner. A change of time at the close of a Rondo is an exception to this rule. Here, particularly in the case of a long extended Rondo-form with episodes of development, a protracted coda is added as a Stretto in accelerated tempo, such as we find, for instance, in Beethoven's Finales in op. 31 and op. 53.

We distinguish two kinds of Rondo-form: I. Rondos without episodes of contrast, whose episodes, as unimportant parts of the movement, must not be repeated no matter whether they be episodes of development or transitory episodes; II. Rondos with episodes of contrast which are often only repeated in part or more frequently only to a certain extent concisely alluded to by suggestion.

We will next present two models, one of each kind and for these choose movements which Beethoven has expressly described as "Rondos". A very distinct idea of the first kind may be gained from a study of the Rondo in Beethoven's Sonata in D major, op. 10. III. The principal subject which is developed from the short motive in Ex. 87

closes upon the first crotchet of the ninth-bar; this is followed by the second portion in D major, which after eight bars proceeds to an eight-bar episode of transition which begins as follows:

The Rondo without Contrasting Episode.

and which comes to a conclusion with a pause on the first inversion of the dominant seventh. After the pause the repetition of the principal subject begins, this closes in B flat major with an interrupted cadence in the ninth-bar. Here we have a transitory part of twelve bars, which ends with a pause, thus.

The third entry of the subject now follows in B flat major and modulates to D minor. This somewhat imperfect entry in a foreign key is to a certain extent the forerunner of the repetition of the whole of the principal part of the Rondo which occurs later in the tonic, D major. The motive of the subject produced in the third bar,

is then employed within the next six bars for the purpose of modulating to D major.

Jadassohn, Manual of Mus. Form.

The perfect repetition of both the first parts of the Rondo are now begun; the second portion progresses to the key of the subdominant and then modulates to B minor. A short episode of development is now added, in which the initial motive of three quavers is employed in the following manner.

The Rondo without Contrasting Episode.

After the pause a new entry of the principal subject is introduced with the following alterations.

93.

An episode of transition developed from the three quaver-motive again follows and proceeds to a chord of the dominant seventh.

The small coda, which follows, is directly developed from the initial motive, with the exception of the modulatory deviation of four bars given in syncopated rhythm.

In this Rondo we see the principal subject occurring five times, and four episodes assist in reproducing it. Of these one is strictly an episode of development but none of them is reproduced even by suggestion. The study of this Rondo in particular is the more easy and instructive for the pupil, because the individual parts of the whole are so frequently bounded by pauses and thereby made more distinct. The Finale of op. 28 and of op. 31. 1, are formed in quite a similar way. They are more extended however and contain a Stretta, as final coda.

The Rondo with Episode of Contrast.

§ 18. For the study of the Rondo with an episode of contrast we select the Finale of Beethoven's A major Sonata, op. 2. II. The subject is given out in the first sixteen bars; and is repeated for the first time in the last sixteen bars previous to the episode of contrast. This episode presents a character totally different to that of the subject, it bears the character of a Trio in dance-form. The repetition of the first portion of this "Trio", as we may call it, is represented by the usual sign, that of the second portion is written out in full, because a modulation of eight bars follows a half close on the dominant; and this modulatory portion is succeeded by the 2nd repetition of the subject, again entering with its sixteen bars in the key of A major. We find the third repetition of the subject in this portion in the same position as we found the first repetition in the first part of the Rondo; in this case however it appears varied for thirteen bars. A further episode of transition, developed from the initial motive in A major, leads after thirteen bars to a second inversion of the chord of B flat. A partial repetition of the Trio for eight bars occurs here, and to this is attached a modulation of four bars to A major. The movement is now brought to a close with a fourth, but somewhat varied repetition of the subject.

The Finale of Beethoven's Sonata in E flat, op. 7, is formed in a similar manner. In this Rondo we find a Trio with two distinct parts, which are both to be repeated. The somewhat free, but partial repetition of the Trio brings the movement to a close in E flat.

It is characteristic of both kinds of Rondo-form that the subject is at times presented in a distant key. This can be seen in the Rondo of the E flat Sonata, op. 7, and also in the Rondo of Beethoven's Concerto in E flat. As a rule, however the foreign key is very quickly quitted, and the classical composer returns again to his principal key after a deviation of a few bars. If the Rondo possesses a real episode of contrast, this must present a distinct antithesis to the principal subject.

The episode of contrast in the Finale of the A major Sonata, op. 2. II, has in comparison with the lovely, cheerful subject, a restless, passionate character. In the Rondo of the E flat Sonata, op. 7, the heroic nature of the episode of contrast stands forward more prominently on account of the tender and graceful character of the first part.

Although most pieces in Rondo-form are written in Allegretto or Allegro moderato, still this form may be employed in slower movements; and although most compositions in this form usually present a cheerful, pleasing initial subject, still there are not wanting those which bear a melancholy or passionate character. We can only call to mind at present the serious Rondo in A minor by Mozart, surely wellknown to all our readers.

The pupil should not endeavour at first to compose extended pieces in the first kind of Rondo-form. Later he may strive to imitate the second kind; for pieces in this form contain within themselves the necessity of prolongation. The pupil will discover many varieties in his studies of the Rondos; but all pieces of this kind will undoubtedly refer themselves back to the two kinds of Rondo-form which we have suggested. The more advanced student may seek to effect a change in his work, by occasionally composing a Rondo for piano and violin. As a pattern to work upon we would suggest Beethoven's Sonata for piano and violin, op. 24, the Finale; but the pupil should of course, carefully study and analyse other Rondos of this kind.

CHAPTER VII.

THE SONATA.

The Form of the Sonata in General.

The Sonata is a musical composition consisting of two or more movements. The individual movements should form a complete musical combination, although their contents differ. An external relationship sometimes exists between the two last movements, if the second last, usually a slow movement, is connected with the last by a direct means of communication. But even without any such means, a composition at times demands an immediate continuation between two of its movements. This is particularly noticeable when the previous movement is of no great length. At the close of the Adagio sostenuto in Beethoven's Sonata in C sharp minor, op. 27. II, we find the injunction, "Attacca subito il seguente", that is to say, begin the following movement at once.

This is not merely the case with movements in the same tonic, as in the previous example C sharp minor and D flat major, but a direct connection is sometimes necessary between movements in different keys. This can happen without a modulatory passage if the final chord of the previous, and the first chord of the following movement will permit. Beethoven's Concerto in G major, op. 58, in the Andante con moto, concludes on a chord of E minor; the immediate continuation is demanded by the words "Segue il rondo", and the Rondo proceeds with its first chord of C, after the chord of E minor is heard fading away. This however must not be accepted too literally, for the first chord of the Rondo must be struck directly after the cessation of the semi-quaver rest in the last bar of the Andante, somewhat in this fashion:

In all such cases, a pause, even if ever so short, say as long as taking a deep breath requires, must be made, and this must happen even if the very last note of the previous movement is prolonged by means of a pause. A short pause — a breathing space — would even in such a case be necessary between the close of one and the commencement of the other movement.

As a general rule a Sonata has three movements, in which case the first and last are written in a rapid tempo, the middle one usually in a slow tempo. Sonatas are to be found with two or four movements and then it does not follow that the first shall be in every instance the quickest. Beethoven's Sonata in A flat, op. 26, has four movements and the first is Andante con variazioni, whilst his Sonata, op. 54, has only two movements, and is superscribed in the first movement "in tempo d'un menuetto", and accordingly proceeds at a moderate pace. A single movement with the title, "Sonate", is to be found in one exceptional instance, whether it be correct or not, we leave an open question; however Moscheles called one of his noblest productions, consisting of a single movement, "Sonate Mélancolique".

Amongst Beethoven's thirty Piano Sonatas we find — the two small Sonatas, op. 49, excepted — only four of them with two movements, and most of them have three as is the rule with similar works of his predecessors. The movements of a Sonata when it contains four of them, are arranged as a rule as follows; the first, quick, the second slow, the third a Scherzo or Minuet and the final movement quick. Beethoven's Sonata, op. 109, in its Finale entitled "Andante molto cantabile ed expressivo", presents a single instance of a final slow movement: still in this Andante con Variazioni the tempo changes and we find two variations in rapid time. On the whole however it is a slow movement and concludes "in tempo 1 del tema". We call this an exceptional case but would give the hint to the pupil that it is the "only" instance. The Arietta con Variazioni in op. 111, is for the most part a quick movement.

At times a Sonata is totally destitute of a slow movement, that is to say, a strict Adagio or Andante; as can be seen in Beethoven's Sonatas op. 10. II; op. 14. I; op. 31. III; op. 78 and op. 90. One of these has no Adagio although it has four movements. We refer to the Sonata op. 31. II which contains an initial movement, marked Allegro, a Scherzo Allegretto vivace, a Minuet moderato e grazioso and a finale presto con fuoco. The Menuetto takes the place of a slow movement, say an Adagio or a strict Andante. The Sonata in F sharp major, op. 78, contains only two movements, after the short Adagio cantabile of four bars, and both are quick movements.

Different Arrangements of the several Movements.

§ 20. The form of the Sonata with three movements is frequently employed in the composition of trios. Mozart has indeed written one of his most beautiful symphonies, that in D major without a Minuet, in only three movements. Should a Sonata in four movements be used in the construction of a composition for a solo instrument or for a combination of instruments or for an orchestra, the position of the middle movements can occasionally be changed in order to have the slow movement second or third. The short, quick movement, whether a Scherzo or Minuet, can just as well precede as follow the slow movement. Beethoven in his Sonata in A flat, op. 26, places a lively Scherzo in front of the Funeral March. The reason for this is easy to see; he would not allow a second slow movement to follow the 'Andante con Variazioni'. Two successive slow movements of any great length would soon prove wearisome.

Sometimes a short Adagio in simple song-form is introduced in the middle of the Sonata, as for example the Adagio con espressione in the Sonata in E flat major, op. 27. I, or we find an extended introduction written in a slow tempo, such as the Adagio molto in op. 53, which is expressly marked "Introduzione". Short Adagios of this sort always connect themselves with the following movement; and Beethoven indeed expressly mentions this in the case of the two Adagios already mentioned, although the immediate continuation is a matter of course, and the remark "Attacca subito l'Allegro" in the one case and "Attacca subito il Rondo" in the other, is superfluous.

Introductory movements of longer or shorter duration, in a slow tempo are of rare occurrence before the first movement of a Sonata. In Beethoven's Piano Sonatas lengthy introductions in slow time only occur in the Sonata Pathétique and in op. 111. That the principal idea of the slow movement can also be reproduced in the first movement, strictly so called, can be seen in the Sonata Pathétique, in Schumann's Quartett in E flat major, op. 47, and in Schubert's C major Symphony.

Shorter slow preludes, of less than eight bars, are seldom met with. Beethoven only employs such a short prelude once, as already mentioned in his Sonata in F sharp major, op. 78. No one would regard the introductory chord in the D minor Sonata, op. 31. II as a prelude.

Occasionally an introductory cadenza is employed before the first movement. Beethoven opens the first movement of his greatest Concerto, that in E flat major, with a passage richly ornamented with the dominant, subdominant and tonic chords. As a rule an introduction to the first movement is not requisite, but under certain circumstances it is necessary: then however it must stand in direct connection with the first movement following it. Sometimes the subject of the first movement is already suggested and prepared in the introduction, whilst a characteristic motive of the subject forms the commencement of the introduction and provides the material for it, as, for example, is the case in the introduction to Schumann's Symphony in B flat major. A motive of this sort may only occasionally occur in the course or towards the close of the introduction. Indeed Beethoven already presents the motive of the second subject in the Allegro movement of both his Leonore overtures, in the introduction.

The contents of the introduction, as a rule, are usually more independent and more freely preparatory to the first movement. Even the Finales of many of the longer works in Sonata-form frequently have a prelude or introduction in slow time before the real quick final movement; these are then worked out on the same principles as the introduction to a first movement, except that they are generally somewhat curtailed.

In the first movement of a Sonata we meet with a new form, which we will describe in a few words and give its outlines in the following manner. The movement consists of three parts, the first containing the two principal subjects, the second comprising the working out, the third is the repetition part, to which is added in works of any great length, a Coda. Before we study the form of a movement of a Sonata so constructed, let us first turn our attention to it in its diminished proportions, as we find them in the Sonatina.

CHAPTER VIII.

THE SONATINA.

The first movement in a major key.

§ 21. The Sonatina is — as its name bespeaks — a short Sonata. At times it consists of only two, at times also of three movements. If the Sonatina consists of only two movements it is not always necessary that the first should be Allegro, and the second Andante or Adagio. Should the Sonatina have three movements it is generaly arranged in the usual form, a quick, a slow, and a final quick movement. The first movement, according to the kind of key in which it is written, presents a different order of modulation. If the major key be employed, the second subject almost always appears in the key of the dominant, with which the first part then concludes. Beethoven however introduces the second subject in another key than that of the dominant in his greater works which contain movements in Sonata-form, and which, in the corresponding movements of his Piano-sonatas, sometimes comprise a second principal idea: but we will return to speak of this later. The first part of one of his larger movements differ substantially in their broader development and more lengthy representation expressing a greater wealth of idea, from the first small Sonatina movements; in general principles however they are formed alike. The first small Sonata movements, even if they have a very important intellectual purport, are quite similar to the Sonatina movements: as can be seen in the first movement of op. 78.

The whole of the first part of the Sonatina is repeated; to this the "working out" part or free fantasia is attached, which should be kept within bounds, and in no way allowed to have an extension similar to that of the first part. There is scarcely

The first movement in a major key. 93

room here for extended contrapuntal device, development of one or another of the principal subjects or motives detached from them must suffice, representing them as varied as possible and then proceeding to the third part of the movement. The third part brings about a repetition of the first part in such a manner that the second subject is reproduced in the key of the tonic so that the movement ends in this key either with or without the addition of a Coda.

If we turn to the first movement of Beethoven's Sonata, or more properly speaking Sonatina, op. 49. II, we shall find the first subject given out in the first four bars.

The bass completes the four bars with three quavers, (g, b, d), after which a repetition of the first period, an octave higher, follows with a richer and more extensive accompaniment.

To this is attached a continuation of two three-bar periods, of which the first closes in the key of the tonic, the second in that of the dominant.

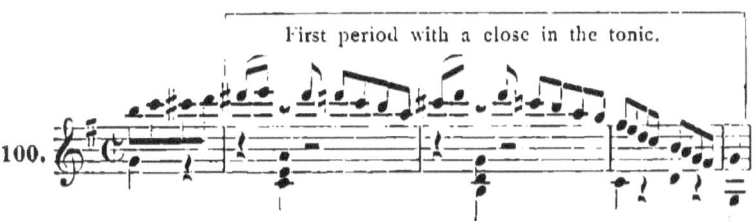

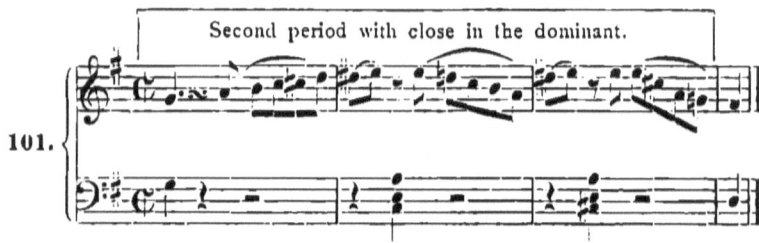

The first subject combined with a second episode of three two-bar phrases now enters; the episode is developed from the figure accompanied with quavers in triplets, and closes at the sixth bar, in which the second subject is taken up in D major, the dominant, at the up-beat of the last triplet. This subject brings its first eight-bar period to a conclusion on the dominant of D major.

Upon its reproduction this period returns to D major, in thirteen bars of an extended close, which, like the episode, is accompanied by quavers in triplets. This is then followed by a Coda of four bars, which is developed from the motion of the episode.

If we look into this Coda more closely, we shall observe that the strict idea of it only extends over one bar. This bar is repeated, and to this is further added a two-fold reproduction of the last crotchet of the first bar of the Coda; the final chord is strengthened by striking the second and third crotchets of the last bar. We find the same principle at work in other Codas; the idea in the Coda repeats immediately and to this is added its final motive. Sometimes the repetitions contain small variations. A striking example of a somewhat extended Coda can be found in the first movement of Beethoven's Sonata in F major, op. 10. II.

96   The Sonatina.

The whole idea in the Coda sometimes repeats more than once, particulary if it be short. An example of this can be found in the Coda of Beethoven's Sonata in F minor, op. 2, I: the idea contained in the Coda only occupies two bars, but is repeated twice and is somewhat lengthened on its second repetition in order to form a close.

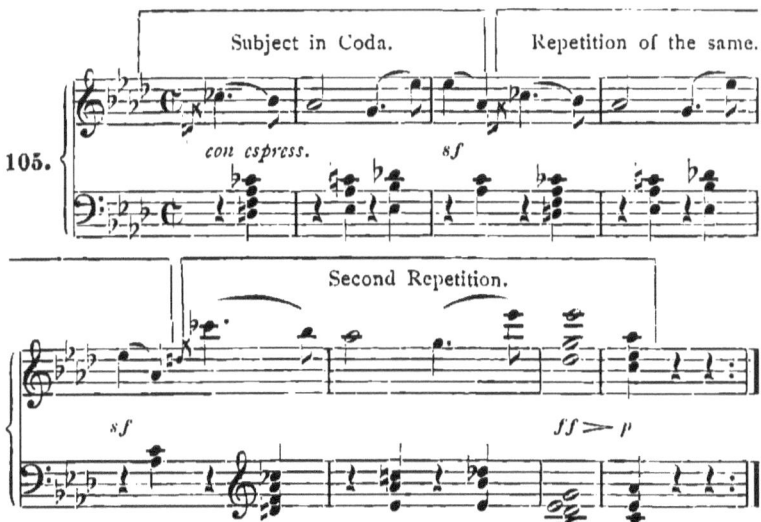

The subject of the Coda, concentrated and shortened, is sometimes repeated several times successively, as for instance in Beethoven's Sonata in G major, op. 31. I.

Among other results however the feeling of termination is produced by the dilatory repetition of the last motive. This is exemplified in the first movement of Beethoven's Sonata in E minor, op. 90.

An independent idea for the Coda is however not always imperative. Beethoven in his Sonata in F sharp major, op. 78, employs a motive from the termination of the second subject for the construction of the Coda, thus.

The first movement in a major key.

In the Coda of example 106 we see the idea alternating repeatedly between minor, major and minor. This is a characteristic quite peculiar to the great master, Beethoven, instances of which are often to be met with in other places. He however does not always allow the whole of the idea in the Coda to change its mode; frequently he only uses the last motive of it for this purpose. This can be seen in the first movement of Beethoven's Sonata in B flat major, op. 22.

7*

100   The Sonatina.

The alteration of g to g flat in the final motive has in this case, the effect of a change from major to minor.

Frequently the reproduction of the final motive is also employed simultaneously with the return to the repetition of the first part or with the introduction of the second: a distinct idea of this may be obtained from the close of the first part of Beethoven's Sonata, op. 53.

The first movement in a major key.

Still more interesting is the repetition at the close of the third part of the first movement, where, upon a complete reproduction of the motive of the Coda, the harmonies of F major and minor enter alternately, and the transposition of the last motive modulates to F minor in the fourth part which forms an extended Coda, and finally brings the movement to a conclusion.

The pupil can easily observe from the figuring of chords in the last example, as well as from all the Codas previously suggested, that manifold repetitions of a full close form the basis of the harmony of a Coda. Let us now return after this deviation to a consideration of the Sonatina in G major, op. 49. II, and obtain a distinct view of the second part. After the close of the first part in D major, the second begins in D minor. We cannot here speak of a strict Free Fantasia or "working out"; it is merely a transposition of the main idea to the minor, without a thematic development in contrapuntal combination entering with the whole idea or a motive from it. Instead of a working out part we find a mere continuation, a further weaving of the movement as a whole, without developing new forms by contrapuntal combinations from one or other of the themes and motives of the first part, or from one of the motives of a theme. The second part, in the present instance, proves much shorter in comparison with the first, because in the strict sense of the word there is no 'working out' but only a two-fold continuation of the first subject; viz: from D minor to A minor and from A minor to the dominant harmony of E minor. After this continuation, occupying six bars, a pedal of four bars duration enters on B, and this contains no trace of any connection with the subjects or the other motives. The figure, developed from the pedal, proceeds by means of the following sequence to the third part.

The third part contains a faithful reproduction of the first, with this difference, that the second subject is now produced in the key of the tonic, G major, and that the Coda is extended by further repetitions for the purposes of developing as perfect a close as possible.

The first movement in a minor key.

§ 22. Should the first movement of a Sonatina begin in a minor key it is regarded as a rule that the second subject should commence in the relative major, and conclude the first part in this key. But the major mode of the minor sixth, as well as the minor mode of the dominant prove themselves equally suitable for the representation of the second subject. The first part then closes in every instance in the same key as that in which the second is written. Beethoven concludes the first part of his Sonata in F minor, op. 57, in A flat minor, after the second subject had entered in A flat major. Not only the episode which follows the second subject and prepares the close of the first part, but also the Coda terminating the part are in A flat minor. In Beethoven's Kreutzer Sonata for piano and violin, op. 47, the second subject is introduced in the first part of the first Allegro movement in the major mode of the dominant, E major, but is soon transposed to E minor, in which the splendid idea at the close is produced.

114.  &c.

The part is closed with a Coda in this key. In the Sonata Pathétique, op. 13, Beethoven introduces the second subject completely in the minor mode of the minor third, E flat minor; E flat major first entering later in the closing portion and in the Coda concluding the first part. This is however an isolated case. The pupil will do best to adhere to the rules and principles previously laid down for him. Upon its repetition in the third part, the older composers usually introduce the second subject, if it had been in a major key, in a minor one. that is to say, in the same key as the first subject, in order by this means to obtain the utmost unity of key in the proportionately small extended form of a first movement. Mozart proceeds thus in his Sonatas in A and C minor and in many other of his greater works, and Beethoven also

The first movement in a minor key. 105

in his small Sonata, op. 49. I, which we at the same time recognise as a Sonatina. Beethoven however departs from this procedure in his later works; and produces the second subject, written in a major mode, upon its repetition in the third part, in the same major mode, or in another corresponding major key, and then returns by a modulation to the principal key of the movement in order to conclude in it. In cases where Beethoven does not at all permit the second subject, no matter whether it stand in the first part in a major or minor key, to be repeated in the same key in the third part of the movement as in the first, still he chooses the best corresponding key for the repetition, that is to say, the subdominant, and then returns to the key of the tonic. To make this thoroughly distinct we give two examples from op. 10. I and from op. 13.

115.

1. First Subject in C minor.

&c.

Second Subject in first part in E flat major.

in third part in F major.

&c.

2nd Subject transposed to C minor in third part.

&c.

106   The Sonatina.

116.

First Subject in C minor.

2nd Subject in first part in E flat minor.

in 3rd part in F minor, modulates to C minor.

2nd Subject later in C minor.

Frequently a first movement in a minor key concludes upon the harsh chord of the major form of the tonic, although the second subject as well as the Coda are written in the minor mode. Beethoven employs this at the close of the first movement of the Sonatina, op. 49. I.

117.

Coda transposed to G minor.

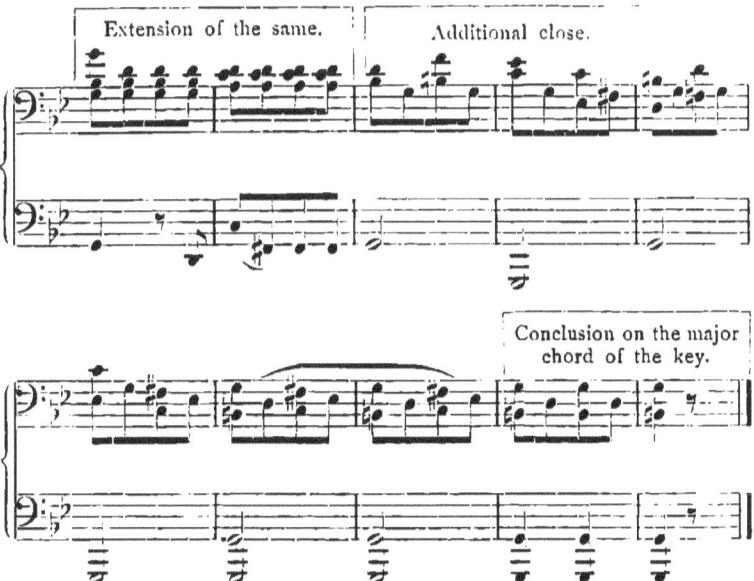

It but rarely happens, that the third part, from where the second subject is transposed into the major, remains completely in this mode; but this occurs in movements of greater breadth than the Sonatina. A termination, such as is shown in the last example, is constantly to be met with. These are the important differences between a minor movement and one in the major. In all other respects they are similarly formed. The second and third movements of a Sonatina are enveloped in forms already known to the student. A Minuet or a short movement written in song-form forms the middle movement, a Rondo the Finale. Beethoven in his Sonatina op. 49. I, presents the first movement in the moderate time of an Andante, whilst the Finale is a lively Rondo in G major. In his next Sonatina, op. 49. II, the first movement is a gay Allegro, whilst the Finale is a stately Minuet, also in G major, but with a Trio in C major consisting of only one part. A movement with variations would not easily adapt itself to the form of a Sonatina, because the variations, even if on a short subject, soon acquire too great a length. Such a movement would be out of proportion then to the other short movements of the whole work.

The Sonatina.

The form of the first movement of a Sonatina adapts itself, although in an exceedingly limited fashion, to the composition of Marches of considerable length by means of the following device. The first movement of the Sonatina forms the principal movement of the March in two parts; then follows a Trio corresponding to the enlarged proportions of a March after which the March and under certain circumstances, the Trio or a part of it repeat: and to this an enlarged Coda is added. In a similar manner a Scherzo can be formed. So then we meet with the smallest possible form of the first movement of a Sonatina in the utmost extension of the dance-form. The pupil should only then first seek to employ these sorts of pieces in mixed forms if he has successfully written a number of Sonatina movements. The beginner will find striking examples for study and analysis in Mozart's Sonatas no. 11, F major; no. 14, G major: no. 15, C major (Peters' Edition), and in Haydn's Sonatinas. Models of the combination of Sonatina-movement and dance-form, which we have just explained above, can be found in the larger Marches of Schubert arranged as duets.

As it is of importance that the pupil should acquire a perfect mastery over the form of the first movement of a Sonatina, he might after successful work for piano solo, compose Sonatinas for piano-duets and even for a Trio of violin, violoncello and piano, so that he should not weary himself with constantly repeating the same work. The pupil thus combines a practice of variety in styles with a study in form and at the same time makes useful preparatory studies for his future attempts at chamber music.

CHAPTER IX.

THE FIRST MOVEMENT OF A SONATA.

The first part of the first movement; the first subject and its connection with the second.

§ 23. We have already remarked that every musical idea regulates its own form according to its intellectual contents. In many pieces we find movements which possess besides the first and second subject, a third subject in the episode connecting them, as well as a Codetta which follows the second subject and moreover contains a new and independent idea, and finally has a Coda-motive for the conclusion of the first part. This would be without doubt the most extended form of a first movement, such as we find for example in Beethoven's Sonata for piano and violin, op. 47. We quote this movement in particular, just to show the pupil unmistakeably what an immense difference there is between a Sonatina and Sonata-movement, so far as the form of the latter with its conditionally extended contents is concerned.

The chief difference between the movement of a Sonatina and Sonata will be found in the fact, that in the latter the ideas, richer and more lavish of contents in themselves, require even upon their first appearance in the first part, a more extended representation: so that the other members of the part, such as the episodes with their concomitant motives and independent ideas, modulatory passages, Codettas and Codas, must be proportionately more significant and extensive. Besides the change from the key of the tonic (for the first subject), the episodes enter in other related keys. In this manner Beethoven introduces to the second subject in the first movement of his Sonata in C major, op. 2. III, beginning with the following bars:

110   The First Movement of a Sonata.

the following independent idea in G minor in an extended episode.

Subject repeated in D minor.

This idea is repeated and concludes with a modulation to A minor; then a transitory episode of five bars leads in the fifth bar to the dominant (D) of the key, in which the second subject, shown in Ex. 118, enters in the first part. Upon the reproduction of both ideas in the third part, the keys of C minor and C major correspond to the keys of G minor and G major in the first part.

In the Sonata, op. 10. III, the first subject in D major is followed by an episode in the relative minor, B minor. This episode contains at the same time a perfectly distinct and independent idea, which repeats within the episode.

112   The First Movement of a Sonata.

A transition immediately leads to a close in A major, in which key the second subject is produced in the first part. We give the commencement of the second subject in Ex. 121

This second subject in its development from the motive

partakes less indeed of the character of a principal idea than that of the episode shown in Ex. 120. Beethoven in his Sonata in D major, op. 28, likewise presents an episode with an independent subject. It begins in F sharp minor as follows:

The second subject in A major does not enter till later.

We also meet with episodes containing independent ideas in the key of the dominant; as an example we give the subject of the episode from Beethoven's Sonata in B flat major, op. 22.

It is impossible to regard this idea as the second subject of the movement, although after an introduction of six bars on a pedal on the Dominant (C), it enters quite naturally in F major and after eight-bar closes in this key; the second subject itself does not appear until after the close of the incidental melody; it commences as follows:

Independent ideas in episodes are also to be met with in the key of the first subject, as is shown in the next example from Beethoven's Sonata for piano and violin, op. 47.

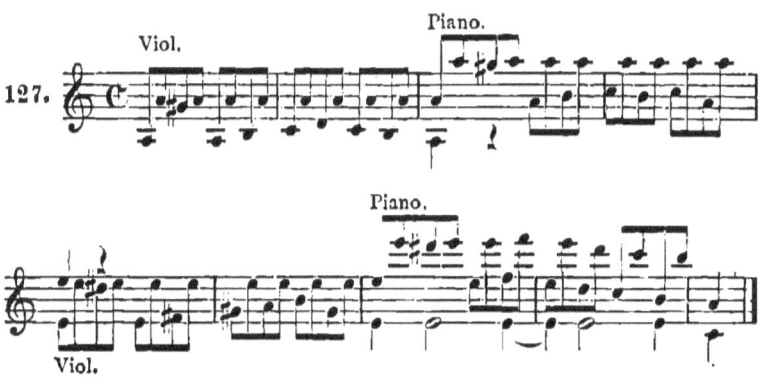

Jadassohn, Manual of Mus. Form.

This idea appears again in the Coda of the first part, but somewhat curtailed.

A similar occurrence is to be found in Beethoven's Piano Sonata, op. 53. The motive occurs in a modulatory episode as follows:

and is found again in the Coda of this part thus —

From the foregoing examples it is evident that independent ideas in the episodes, can be introduced in the same or nearly related keys of both subjects. Ideas or motives of an independent character, which are to be found in an episode occupying a position between the second subject and the Coda, are always placed like the Coda itself, in the key of the second subject. Episodes of this sort always bear in themselves the character of a Codetta, as we call it, in distinction to the Coda. In individual instances we even find two Codas at the close of the first part; as the pupil can see in the last thirteen bars of the first part of the first movement of Beethoven's Sonata in B flat major, op. 22.

The Modulation after the First Subject.

§ 24. It appears from what has already been said that there are Sonata-movements which contain other independent ideas in the first part besides the two subjects, but this however is by no means a necessary condition of the Sonata. In Beethoven's Sonatas we find movements of short, moderate and very great extension, which only possess two subjects and a limited form of Coda. The first parts of his Sonatas op. 2, 1, op. 53, op. 90 and op. 106 are of very varied lengths but still they only contain two subjects. The Sonata, op. 53, presents an idea in the Coda, developed from the motive occurring in a transitory episode, such as we have shown in Exs. 129 and 130. This principle, of presenting only two themes, Beethoven adheres to most firmly in by far the greatest number of his compositions in Sonata-form, and does not even forsake it in his most important and extensive works for the piano, for a combination of instruments or even for the orchestra itself. The manner in which he introduces his subjects, how he employs them in connection with one another, in what keys he places the second subject, over and above the key of the dominant employed in a movement in a major key, these are some of the points upon which we will seek to obtain a nearer view. We have already remarked that Beethoven very rarely and exceptionally inserts lengthy introductions in a slow tempo before the first movement, strictly so called, in his pianoforte Sonatas, or even in his Sonatas for piano and violin. We will at once take up the consideration of

The First Subject.

Beethoven sometimes only allows the characteristic motive of the subject to enter first, and brings this to a termination with a pause, as we see in Sonata, op. 111:

or in the Symphony in C minor.

In his Sonata, op. 106 the motive is immediately repeated a third higher.

All three motives are vividly expressed; and the pause upon the last note of the motive, or after it, as it is shown in the previous example, allow the audience to retain the motive firmly in their memory. Beethoven frequently lets a pause follow upon a rest after the first subject has been given out, or upon the last note of the subject. This is exemplified in the following pianoforte Sonatas: op. 2. I; op. 10. III; op. 31. I, II and III; op. 53, op. 57, op. 90, op. 101, and op. 106, as well as in the Sonata for violin and piano, op. 47, the C minor and A major Symphonies and in other works. It has almost the appearance as if Beethoven convinced of the vast importance and intrinsic value of his ideas, allowed the audience time to grasp the main idea of his first movement and to impress it upon themselves. As a rule a short repetition of the subject then follows and its continuation to the dominant harmony of such key as the second subject may be presented in. It is characteristic of Beethoven that in this modulatory episode he almost invariably leaves the key of the movement immediately, and hastens as rapidly as possible to his desired dominant harmony.

Reluctant as we undoubtedly are to make use of plans of musical forms at any great length, still we will employ numbers in this exceptional instance to show the pupil in how far our assertion is correct. In the annexed table, which is merely intended to assist in aiding his analysis of the first part of the first movements of Beethoven's Sonatas, we present him with many striking examples.

The Modulation after the First Subject.   117

Sonata	Length of the first part.	Point of departure from the tonic.	Entry of the Dominant-harmony.
op. 2. I. M. I.	48 bars.	9th bar.	20th bar.
op. 2. I. M. IV.	56 ,,	11th ,,	12th ,,
op. 2. II. M. I.	116 ,,	38th ,,	42nd ,,
op. 7. M. I.	136 ,,	25th ,,	35th ,,
op. 10. I. M. I.	105 ,,	32nd ,,	48th ,,
op. 13. M. I.	122 ,,	28th ,,	33rd ,,
op. 14. I. M. I.	60 ,,	17th ,,	17th ,,
op. 14. II. M. I.	63 ,,	14th ,,	14th ,,
op. 22. M. I.	68 ,,	13th ,,	16th ,,
op. 27. II. M. III.	63 ,,	16th ,,	18th ,,
op. 28. M. I.	161 ,,	39th ,,	41st ,,
op. 31. II. M. I.	92 ,,	31st ,,	31st ,,
op. 53. M. I.	83 ,,	19th ,,	23rd ,,
op. 57.	64	24th ,,	24th ,,
op. 30. II.	74 ,,	27th ,,	28th ,,

We might enlarge this table considerably with quotations from the numerous works of the great master, but in this case it suffices, even if in an abridged fashion, to act as a necessary sign-post to the student. In the analysis of the movements of Beethoven's Sonatas with their variety of styles, proofs of our assertion can be constantly found. Frequently the episode modulating to the desired dominant chord terminates with a more or less broadly developed pedal, from which a passage of perhaps only a few notes leads up to the second subject. We annex a corresponding example from op. 47, movement I.

Similar preparations of the second subject or of a subject occurring in the key of the dominant in a transitory episode before the entry of the idea in the second subject, or of a motive introduced by a pedal, constantly occur in Beethoven's works; for example in the first movement of op. 7. bars 35—39; op. 10. I, bars 48—50; op. 13. bars 34—40; op. 14. I, bars 17 to 21; op. 14. II, bars 19—24; op. 22, bars 16—21; op. 53, bars 23—29; op. 57, bars 24—35, and in many other works.

At times Beethoven places the modulatory episode in the tonic; this episode is in most cases found to be very short, and proceeds at once to the key of the dominant, in which the second subject occurs, as in the first movement of op. 30.

The Modulation after the First Subject.

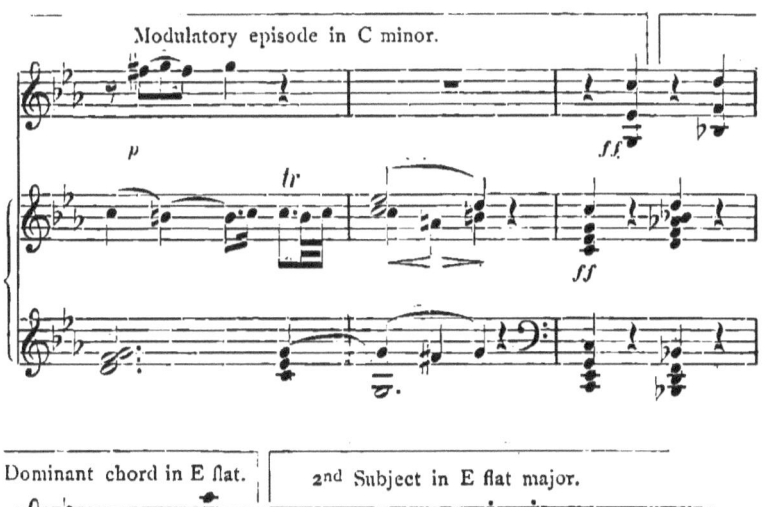

In other cases, where a strict modulatory episode with an idea or motive of an independent character is wanting, Beethoven developes the modulation to the second subject from a motive of the first. But in such cases we always see the effort to strike as soon as possible the dominant harmony of that key in which the second subject shall enter, and to leave what has preceded it at once. To shew this, we add examples taken from op. 31. I and III.

136.

120   The First Movement of a Sonata.

Beethoven proceeds in a similar manner in the first movement of his Symphony in C minor and other works. From all that we have previously said it is surely evident that the *head of the first part*, if we may be allowed the expression, that is, the first subject with the modulatory episode, in case there should be one, only occupies the smaller half of the first part; that in case of a lengthy modulatory episode, this should either be in the key of the dominant as shown in Ex. 125, or in the same as the second subject, in case this is not given in the key of the dominant, as shown in Ex. 129, or in another key nearly related either to the first or second subject, as can be seen in examples 120 and 123. In most cases Beethoven sets the first part in motion after the production of the first subject more in another key than in that employed at the commencement, even if its episode should follow in the same key. Let us now turn our attention to

The Second Subject.

§ 25. This should, even if it bears some internal relationship to the first subject, still present a contrast to it. We need not insert a diffusive discussion here, nor is it necessary to tabulate our proofs. Wherever the pupil only seeks, there he will find by studying the works of the masters, that the second subject bears in itself a character entirely distinct from that of the first; and this is even the case when a motive of the first subject is employed in the construction of the second, as in the first movement of Beethoven's Sonata, op. 57:

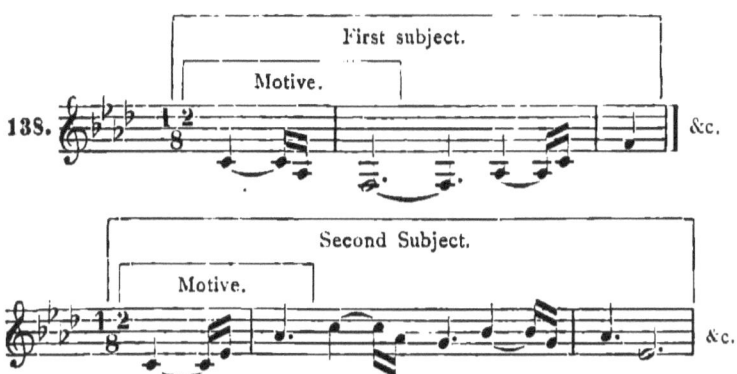

or, when the motive of the first subject enters as an accompaniment to the second, as in the fifth of Beethoven's symphonies.

In a movement in a minor key the change from the minor of the first subject to the relative major of the second always carries its own contrast. This change of key cannot occur in a major movement: in the repetition of the first part after the Free Fantasia, both subjects moreover would appear for the most part in the same key. The contrast between the subjects should never be harsh or violently forced. The internal relationship of both is represented in most of the best works of the masters by the fact that they are written in the same tempo. Any important difference in tempo between the two subjects would disturb the organic structure of the whole; small, unnoticeable *nuances* would not have this effect, these, as a rule, are not written out, and it is left to the taste and feeling of the performer or conductor, to decide whether and where he shall allow the same to enter. We have not the slightest intention of speaking of the willingness with which many performers give expression to their superabundance of feeling, and still less of approving of the arbitrary, unwritten alteration in the tempo of both subjects which, even to-day, many virtuoso-conductors, no matter on what grounds, take a delight in. The noble heights of the true masterpieces need no such interpretation and do not even suffer it. The movements of such works proceed as a rule, ritardandos and pauses excluded, in the same tempo and are so most correctly represented.

We have already mentioned in the explanation of the first part of the Sonatina, that the second subject of a movement in a minor key can be placed in various keys. But the second subject in a major movement may also be produced in the first part in another key than that of the dominant. In Beethoven's Sonata in C, op. 53, we find the second subject in E major, and similarly the second subject of the Sonata in G major, op. 31. I, in B major. This is not a rare occurrence; in both instances just mentioned the Coda is given in the minor. Even in the G major Sonata, a transposition of the second subject from B major to B minor can be found already in the ninth bar. In the two great Leonore Overtures, Nos. 2 and 3, the first subject enters in C major, the second in E major, in

The Modulation after the Second Subject.

which major key the first part concludes. Example 140 shows the final chord of the first part and the bars introducing the Free Fantasia of the Leonore Overture, No. 3.

In the Hammer-Clavier Sonata op. 106, Beethoven produces the second subject in the key of the major sixth; this is immediately followed by the charming final episode in G major;

an abridged Coda is added to the above with a full close in G major.

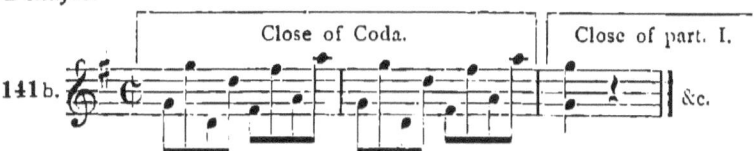

Schubert in his C major symphony, at first introduces the second subject in the minor key of the major third, the relative minor of G major.

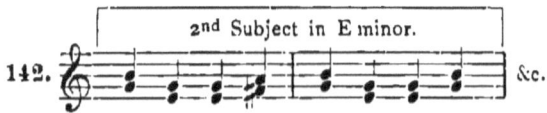

Afterwards he employs it in G major and closes the first part in the key of the dominant. We mention this as an exceptional case. To allow the second subject to enter in the key of the subdominant as in the first movement of Raff's Wald Symphony, or in a minor movement to enter in the major mode of the tonic as in Chopin's E minor Concerto, we regard as a totally unnatural proceeding. We have as little right to harbour the idea of giving the whole of the second subject and the close of the first part in a minor movement, in the major key of the dominant. On the other hand we see the same subject in a minor key placed in the minor mode of the dominant, in which key the first part then terminates. This occurs for example in the D minor Sonata op. 31. II, in the first as well as the third movement, and in the E minor Sonata, op. 90, and in other works, both of Beethoven and other masters.

In the majority of cases we find the second subject in a major movement in the key of the dominant, after that almost solely in the key of the major third; in a minor movement, usually in the relative major, more seldom in the minor mode of the dominant. The pupil will observe that we, neither here nor in other places, wish to lay down hard and fast rules. We suggest from the works of the great master that which has given us proof of his genius; we feel this to be the Correct and the Truth and we merely hint at what we have found in the classical masterpieces.

The Coda in the First Part.

§ 26. Nevertheless the second subject proceeds directly to the Coda in very few cases, and only then if the first part is very short. An episode is found, as a rule, between the end of the second subject and the Coda, which we have called the Codetta. This Codetta contains at times an independent idea or motive. In Sonatas for the piano it is frequently represented in

The Coda in the First Part.

the form of rapid arpeggio-passages. In Sonatas of greater length two such Codettas can succeed each other and to these a Coda may even be added. This can be seen in the next example, taken from Beethoven's Sonata in E flat major, op. 7.

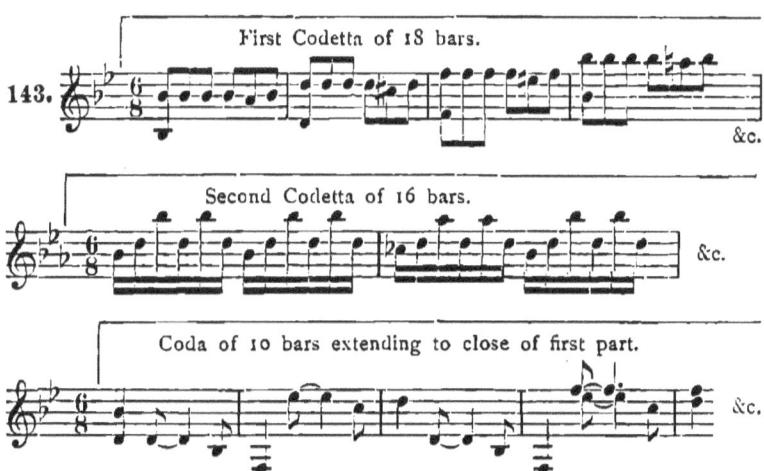

The C major Sonata, op. 53, has in the first part only one Codetta, somewhat broadly worked out in twenty four bars, in the form of an agitated passage on the harmonies of a cadence extending over the chords of the first, fifth, first, fourth and sixth degrees of the scale. It commences as follows.

The Sonata in F minor, op. 57, has a Codetta of ten bars which is succeeded by a Coda of four.

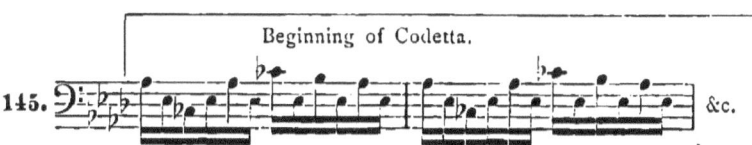

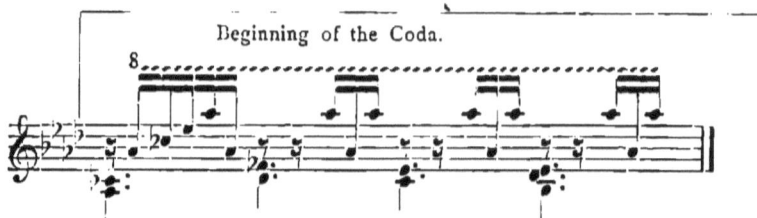

Beginning of the Coda.

The shorter Sonata-forms in op. 78 and op. 90 possess no Codetta. The F sharp major Sonata op. 78 developes its Coda from the final Motive of the second subject, as has already been mentioned in Ex. 108. The E minor Sonata, op. 90, adds an independent Coda immediately upon close of the second subject.

146. Close of 2nd Subject. Beginning of Coda.
&c.

Concerning the Coda concluding the first part we have already said sufficient in the seventh chapter. It only remains still to be mentioned that the first part of a Sonata contains no contrapuntal development, because it has really only to give out the subjects, from which the Free Fantasia in the second part is formed. It is possible to form another new idea in the first part, by connecting a previous subject by means of a motive from the same; otherwise a subject or motive should not be presented in contrapuntal combination, repeated with a thematic development and introduced in a manner similar to that which occurs in the Free Fantasia. This does not hold good merely of Sonatas for the piano or piano and violin, but also for all those movements in chamber music and symphonies, which are written in "Sonata Form". An independent polyphonic tendency of the parts is by no means excluded under these conditions. Throughout the first part of a string-quartett, the parts for the violins, violas and violoncello should not merely be considered as the means for an accompaniment, but they, taking an important part in the representation of the ideas, should make known their qualifications as factors of the whole. It can indeed frequently be seen in the works of the masters, that, even in the first part of a Sonata for the piano, the parts can be independently treated by themselves without intending or effecting a contrapuntal development of the subject, or even of a motive. We meet with various parts, treated independently, and employed simultaneously with the announcement of an idea and taking a part in it. Beethoven's Sonata, op. 2. II, yields a good example.

147.

&c.

In order not to be misunderstood we must still add that the pupil even in the first part, has not anxiously to shun or renounce everything in the shape of a contrapuntal device, or has carefully to avoid the employment of imitation or an inversion of the parts. On the contrary we find just this in the best works of the masters, still always only in such a manner that the clearness of the exposition of the subjects is in no way restricted by it, and so that the exposition is given in a style, at once brief, curt and concise.

CHAPTER X.

THE SECOND PART OF THE FIRST MOVEMENT.

The Free Fantasia.

§ 27. In this part new forms are to be developed from one or more ideas taken from the first part, or even from only one of the motives of the two subjects. The Free Fantasia thus leaves the key in which the first part was written as soon as possible, and, after a number of modulations and after it has touched upon a more or less great variety of keys, returns towards its close to that key from which the third part, a repetition of the first, can be taken up. In by far the greatest number of cases this key is the dominant, since the third part should begin again in the tonic. The keys employed in this part may either be related or distantly removed from those found in the first part; a fixed order of modulation such as could be given for the first part, is not to be thought of here; this is entirely deferred to the taste of the author. Nevertheless the modulation towards the close of the second part must lead in a fluent and appropriate manner to the key of the dominant, or to a chord of the dominant seventh in the key of the tonic, so that the latter may enter as naturally as possible. In order not to weaken the effect of this entrance, it would be as well to allow the key of the tonic to enter neither in the middle of the Free Fantasia, nor still less toward the close of it; as it would have the appearance of the prevailing key in too lengthy a section.

In every Free Fantasia, if only of moderate duration, the key is seldom retained for any length of time, but is changed and by means of the modulation a heightened interest is aroused. The pupil must not think that he can effect this only by modulation, that is by a mere succession of one or more subjects strung together in several different unrelated keys. He would thereby create nothing new but only represent what had gone before, in another selection of keys. Should he wish to employ or make use of the themes and motives at his disposal correctly, he can alone do it by thematic device.

The student well-versed in counterpoint, knows that a piece written in double, triple or quadruple counterpoint or in counterpoint in the tenth or twelfth, often presents a substantially different appearance in its various inversions, although the material is unchanged. This occurs even more frequently in the fugue. A different tone-picture is obtained from the same subject, according as we adopt free or strict parts with the subject, or whether we place the subject in the soprano, bass, or one of the middle parts, and the counterpoints change places with the subject. Even in the working out of a fugue after the first entry of the subject and answer in the keys of the tonic and dominant, we allude again to other keys, undoubtedly in most cases only to such as are nearly related to the tonic. We allow a subject to enter in a major key which was originally conceived in a minor one, in a double fugue we add another subject, the countersubject; in short, in spite of the reasonably strict economy which should prevail in the fugue, we create, from one subject, from one material, varied tone-pictures which yield an organic whole.

Similarly but with a far greater freedom than is possible in the strict form of the fugue, we proceed in the second part of a sonata-movement. In the first place we have a far richer material at our disposal; we can choose between one, two or indeed several ideas contained in the first part. There is left for us the order in which we will thematically develope one or more ideas. We are moreover in no way bound by the fetters of the strict style; we make use of an interchange of the free and the strict style just as it seems suitable for our artistic inspiration, design and purpose.

If we turn to the Free Fantasias of the works of the best masters, we are at once struck by the fact that by no means all the subjects and motives of the first part are employed in the second; nay, that as a rule, only one subject, often only a motive, at times even only the rhythm of a motive, provides the material out of which the Free Fantasia is formed. This subject or the motive derived from it, usually proves to be the initial subject of the movement. Thus we see that the Free Fantasia in Beethoven's fifth Symphony is formed from the initial motive. In his fourth Symphony the first subject and its initial motive,

also provide the material for the second part. The Free Fantasia in the first movement of the seventh Symphony is entirely formed from this rhythm ; the second part of the Sonata in B flat, op. 106, is almost entirely developed from the following motive.

In all these Free Fantasias only one motive is made use of for the real thematic development. The motive indeed, be it ever so short in itself, is divided up into parts each of which is employed alone. This occurs in the first movement of the Sonata in B flat major, op. 106, where not the first rhythm but the second is also employed both in conjunction and individually. Beethoven proceeds in a similar manner with the motive suggested in Ex. 148. After the first four-bar period of the first subject, (in the fourth Symphony), has been employed in the working out, this portion of the motive succeeds:

and afterwards a new melody is added to the first period of the subject.

151.

This is imitated in G minor and E flat major and then proceeds to the entry of the first period (E flat ff). That in the Free Fantasia we do not hear the second period of the first subject in conjunction with the first, produces a marvellous effect. It occurs first at the close of the second part by itself;

152.

and proceeds by means of a chord of the augmented sixth to the second inversion of the chord of the tonic, B flat. Thence the initial motive in an ever increasing course, leads on alone to the re-entry of the first subject in B flat major, with which the third part of the movement begins. The conclusion of the second part is in so far substantially altered from the terminations of other Free Fantasias, that the key of the dominant is not previously heard, and that of the tonic does not even enter for twenty eight bars before the commencement of the third part.

With reference to the Free Fantasia Beethoven appears to us as a discoverer, and in this respect we have to thank him for the more perfect construction of this form. The Free Fantasia of the older writers is, as a rule, substantially shorter than the first part, with Beethoven, in his longer and more important works, we find it little shorter than the first part which is usually of a very concise form. In Beethoven's Piano Sonatas we find the Free Fantasias usually shorter and scantier than in his lengthier works for chamber music and orchestra. This is easily explained by the circumstance, that a movement upon the piano with thematic development must necessarily have narrower limits than would be the case with a string quartett or orchestra. Even taking into consideration the somewhat highly developed technique in the beginning of the present century, Beethoven's genius always paid due regard to the performer; his piano compositions seldom present extraordinary difficulties or such as cannot be overcome.

His longer Sonatas, Trios and Concertos are indeed among the most brilliant and grateful works written for the piano; and reward the performer for his untiring zeal, not merely by the highly aesthetic enjoyment which they yield, but by the fact that they clearly display the perceptive faculties, the dexterity, the technique and bravura of the pianist.

But in the Free Fantasias of Beethoven's Piano Sonatas we are always conscious of the principle of thematic development, they are never mere modulations leading to the repetition of the first part. They always represent a prominently characteristic part of the whole movement and frequently terminate with a pedal, after which the introduction of the third part is then given. Even in his very first Sonatas Beethoven does not shrink from passages difficult of execution, if this is brought about by the thematic development in the Free Fantasia; he always retains what is moderately within the means of a movement for the piano. We suggest, in proof thereof, a passage from the Free Fantasia of the second of the Piano Sonatas, (op. 2. II). In this part the beginning of the initial motive is employed in thematic combination with the initial motive of the first episode. To avoid any oversight we will represent the two motives employed as Motive I and II.

134   The Second Part of the First Movement.

Pedal on the Dominant of A.

Augmentation of triplet figure in second Motive.

Various Commencements of the Free Fantasia.

§ 28. We have already remarked that the second part usually commences in another key than that in which the first part closes; this change of key occasionally takes place unaided, as in the following example from Beethoven's Sonata in E flat major, op. 7.

An example of how it occurs when assisted, can be seen in the next example, from the Sonata in A major, op. 2. II.

The Second Part of the First Movement.

155.

In both cases the Free Fantasia begins with the main motive of the first subject, or with a representation of the first subject in an unrelated key, from which the thematic development of the initial motive afterwards proceeds, as can be seen in Ex. 155 or in the continuation of the same Free Fantasia in Ex. 153.

It is by no means always the case that the first subject or its initial motive commences the second part; this is sometimes connected with the Coda which it continues. The first subject is mostly made use of for thematic development, or frequently, by preference, only its main motive; still there are not wanting instances to the contrary. In the Free Fantasia of Beethoven's B flat major Sonata, op. 22, the initial motive of the movement only appears in the two first introductory bars; on the other hand the motives of the two ideas in the Coda in the first part are employed for thematic device, whilst the figure in ascending chords occurring in the first part, is then employed for the structure of a modulation which leads to the dominant chord of B flat major. In this Free Fantasia nothing is to be found of the second subject, either in the form of rhythm or melody. This is however by no means necessary; very many Free Fantasias contain no trace of the second subject, in others the first is not to be found. Let the student study the second part of the first and last movements of Beethoven's fifth Symphony. In the first movement the Free Fantasia contains no sign of the second subject, whereas in the last no mention is made of the first.

It is impossible to give distinct rules on this point and we can only make this observation, that in the Free Fantasias of the masters, before the entrance of the strict thematic combinations, the subject, from which a motive is afterwards taken for thematic device, is usually introduced again, at first intact but in a different key from that of the first part. In the continuation it appears abridged, for only a portion of the subject is continued until the strict contrapuntal work enters with the motive alone. In contrast to this, the real second part in the Sonata in B flat major, op. 106, begins with strict contrapuntal work, but the Free Fantasia is connected with the repetition of the Coda of the first part, now transposed to a minor key. The motive of the work is re-called by a twofold repetition.

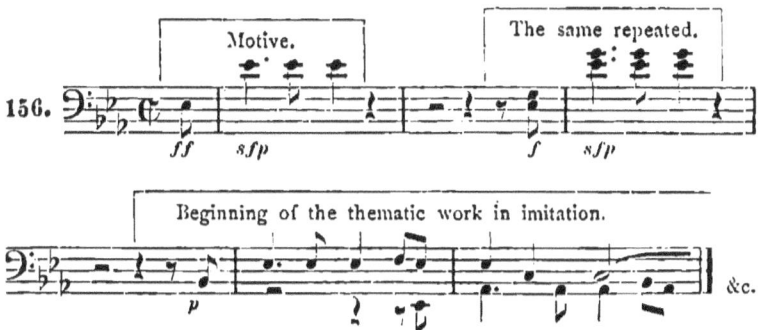

It would carry us far beyond the narrow limits of this textbook, if we were to endeavour to give anything approaching an exhaustive account of the various different Free Fantasias of the classical masters. We however consider the indications already given, as entirely sufficient as a guide-post in the pupil's analysis of the classical works, to throw a light upon, and give an explanation of many details within them, to lead and to support him in the studies appertaining to them. Everybody, the most talented included, must for a long time surrender himself to a careful study of the works of our hero before he can hope to obtain a distinct knowledge of their substance and organism. Then the student can first discover whether he sufficiently possesses the receptivity, the real talent for composition to imitate unwittingly these forms; whether indeed he really possesses such ideas as bear in themselves a germ capable of being developed in these forms. Not every one who, perhaps with ease, can conceive a melodious song or a graceful piano piece in a short form, possesses the talent requisite for the structure of a Sonata, Quartet or Symphony; but still each one's taste for nobler works is aroused and incited by a careful examination of the works of the masters. The reward of such earnest study then will always be a heightened, increased and pleasanter enjoyment of Art.

CHAPTER XI.

THE THIRD PART OF THE MOVEMENT AND THE EXTENDED CODA; THE REMAINING MOVEMENTS OF A SONATA.

The Key of the Second Subject in the Third Part.

§ 29. The third part of a Sonata movement produces then only a repetition of the first part, in such a way that both subjects are written in the same key, the tonic; in other words the second subject in the third part is found in the key of the tonic. This part then proceeds to its end in the tonic, and even if an extended Coda, which really amounts to a movement in Coda, is added, still the third part even then closes in the tonic, even should the "Coda-movement" commence afresh in another key and modulating, touch upon other keys unrelated to the tonic. Of course the final close of the movement must be always in the key of the tonic. Even in the single instance which Beethoven has given in his piano Sonatas, where the second subject in the first part appears in the major sixth (op. 106), the second subject as well as the extended Coda following it appear upon the repetition in the third part in the tonic, B flat major. Moreover all those episodes, found in the first part in the key of the tonic or dominant, which precede the second subject, appear, in the third part, in the key of the tonic.

It is quite another matter if the episodes occur neither in the tonic nor dominant. The episode from Beethoven's D major Sonata, op. 10. III, see Ex. 120, occurs in the third part of the movement in E minor, and proceeds by another modulation at the close to D major, in which key the second subject then appears. The episode from op. 28 in Ex. 123 is produced, upon its reproduction in the third part of the movement, in B minor.

If the second subject in the first part is in the key of the major third, Beethoven reproduces it first in the key of the major sixth and afterwards in the key of the tonic. The pupil can compare the first movements of op. 31. I, and op. 53. On the other hand in the third Leonore Overture he allows the second subject, which originally occurred in E major, to reappear in the third part in the key of C major, the tonic. Perhaps this was done in order to retain a similar instrumental combination, in the first instance double basses, horns, violins and flutes, in the second, the same instruments with the addition of a clarinet. In the Allegro movement of the Leonore Overture No. 2, the second subject is not repeated; the pupil must refer to what has been said on this point in paragraph 29.

140   The Third Part of the Movement and the extended Coda; &c.

Schubert, in the first part of the first movement of his Symphony in C major, allows the second subject to enter in E minor, upon its reproduction he places it first in C minor, afterwards in A minor and finally produces it in the tonic.

In a movement in a minor key, we find a variety of methods of reproducing the second subject in the third part. We have already observed, that the older masters usually transposed it into the minor, if in the first part it appeared in the major, par. 22). Mozart treats his A minor Sonata, the first and last movements of his C minor Sonata, the last movement of his G minor Symphony and many other of his works, in this way. We show the beginning of such a transposition in the following examples taken from his above mentioned Sonatas.

157.

The Key of the Second Subject in the Third Part.

158.

142 The Third Part of the Movement and the extended Coda; &c.

159.

[musical examples: Second Subject in part I, in relative major. / Return of same in part III to original key. / Second Subject in part I &c. / Return of same in part III &c.]

This appears natural in the proportionately very small movements of the older masters and gives the third part a perfect unity of key. This is so much the more important, since the movements usually lack an extended Coda. Beethoven however soon deviates from his predecessors. For, in the first part of his Sonata in C minor, op. 10. I, he introduces his second subject in E flat major, which in the third part is first found in F major and then in its further course it is transposed to C minor. Even this short Sonata movement requires a Coda of greater extension than that in the first part, and so the transposition of part of the second subject and the small Coda is readily explained. Beethoven, in the Sonata Pathétique, avoids the deviation to D flat major, which occurs in the second subject in the first part; he shortens this subject and places it at once in C minor, in which key the episode of the Codetta as well as the Coda itself are introduced. Four bars from the Introduction are now repeated and a final Coda, Allegro con brio, is added. In the F minor Sonata, op. 57, the second subject, which in the first part occurs in A flat major, is repeated in the third part in F major; this subject is then employed in the extended Coda in D flat major, but soon leaves that key. The initial motive of the first two bars is similarly employed at the commencement of the Stretta in F minor. The second subject in the Sonata in C minor, op. 111, which in the first part is in the key of A flat major, is reproduced in C major in the third part. The second subject in Beethoven's other Sonatas in minor keys are employed in the first part in the minor mode of the dominant and are repeated in the third part in the key of the tonic. The movements of the longer Sonatas referred to, are op. 27. II, third movement, op. 31, first and third movements, and op. 90 first movement. In the Sonata for piano and violin in C minor, op. 30, the second subject, originally in E flat major, is reproduced in the third part in C major, to this follows the Codetta, in E flat major in the first part, now transposed to C minor, and finally an extended Coda is added, in E flat major with the characteristics of a Free Fantasia and also beginning in C major. In the Sonata for piano and violin, op. 47, Beethoven places the second subject, which on its first appearance was in the key of E major, in A major on its reproduction in the third part. The close of that part as well as of the whole movement in A minor, is then naturally arranged.

Contraction of the first Subject in the third Part.

§ 30. We find in very many cases at the beginning of the third part, the first subject in an abridged, contracted form. A repetition of a main idea which was introduced at the commencement of the movement, is omitted and the passage to the episode or to the second subject is brought about somewhat more quickly. This occurs in the first movements of Beethoven's Sonatas op. 2. II; op. 2. III; op. 7; op. 10. I; op. 10. II; op. 14. I; op. 31. I and II, and in many other works. Sometimes the third part is shortened by omitting an episode. An instance of this occurs in the first movement of Sonata op. 2. III. The episode, which occurs at the close of the first subject in the first part, is entirely wanting in the third part.

Its omission at this point appears so much the more natural, because the motive of this episode is employed in the episode of the Codetta after the second subject. This latter episode is then repeated in the third part. It begins as follows:

In the first movement of op. 7, the motive occurring at the commencement of the movement after the first subject, is not to be found in the repetition in the third part;

but the modulation by the chord of the dominant seventh,

follows the continuation of the first subject directly, but in a somewhat abridged form.

It is especially characteristic of Beethoven that, upon a repetition of one and the same idea — apart from the modulation to the second subject necessary to the third part, — he seldom, in his later works hardly ever, allows an exact reproduction of a theme as it appeared in the first part. This master seems almost to despise reproducing or copying exactly what he has previously written. He alters the appearance of the idea without changing the idea itself; he adorns and decorates it, employs it with fresh combinations, and thereby makes the repetition of the same idea more interesting than is the case with those of the older masters, whose frequent exact reproductions at times assume a somewhat stereotyped character.

Beyond Beethoven's desire not to copy, this habit explains the occasional extension of the main idea upon its reproduction in the third part. Such a prolongation moreover, we only find as an exceptional case in the first movement of the Sonata in C major, op. 53. In general and especially where the exposition of the first subjects are very extended, contractions are mostly to be found upon a reproduction in the third part.

In the case of the second subject with its auxiliary episodes, abridgments are seldom to be met with on its reproduction in the third part. The Coda of the first part, in case it forms the close in the repetition, would indeed be lengthened as a rule, in order to give the impression of a perfect close. This has already been referred to in analysing the Sonatina-movement. In Beethoven's works however we also find some Sonata-movements, whose third part forms the close of the whole without any such lengthening of the Coda, or even without any advanced extension of the Coda-part. These works, on the one hand are from the first period of Beethoven's life, in which he still worked on the lines of his precursors; on the other hand are such movements as have at the close of the first part a long Coda, or even two. Of such are the first movements of the Sonatas op. 2. II; op. 10. I; op. 2 and op. 22.

The Extended Coda.

§ 31. The third part receives an important enlargement by the addition of the Extended Coda. We could, and perhaps not without reason, call the extended Coda a fourth part of the movement, at least in the works belonging to Beethoven's second and third period; because at times it assumes such immense dimensions, and introduces so much that is new to us in contrapuntal device and in a repeatedly different exposition of the ideas contained in the movement. Even towards the close of the first movement of the ninth Symphony a new idea is brought forward full of tragic earnestness.

164.

Among the protracted Codas by Beethoven we distinguish two kinds according to their different construction. Some contain an exposition of an idea from the previous movement in a Stretta, and this exposition is usually in a more rapid tempo and somewhat altered, with an increased final cadence but no contrapuntal development; the others contain a repeated, small Free Fantasia in contrapuntal combination before they introduce the Final Cadence. The former kind is to be found in extended Rondo-form, (Beethoven's Sonata op. 53, third movement). We meet with them more rarely in the lengthier Sonatas, but the pupil will find an example at the close of the first movement of op. 57. The second sort of extended Coda is more frequently

The Extended Coda.

to be met with not only in the movements of Sonatas, but especially in movements of chamber and orchestral music, written in this form, both by Beethoven and his successors. It will suffice to call the pupil's attention to the first movements of Beethoven's Sonatas op. 53, op. 30 and op. 47.

At times we also find a Coda extended in such a manner that a repetition of a main idea or a motive, with or without contrapuntal development, is added to the third part, after which (in Piano Sonatas, frequently after a Cadence containing more or less brilliant passages), the small Coda of the first part transposed into the tonic, follows and forms the close of the whole movement. As examples we would suggest the first movement of Sonata op. 2. III, and the third movement of Sonata op. 27. II.

Of the remaining movements of a Sonata, the Final one is usually in the same form as the first, but not unfrequently in extended Rondo-form. The form of the Scherzo and Minuet is already known to the student. The slow movement can either be in combined Song-form or Variation-form. Even very extended Dance-forms may be employed. (Beethoven's Funeral March, op. 26.)

We add for the sake of completion that, in chamber and orchestral works, the form of the Sonata usually attains a greater length than in the piano Sonata proper or the Sonata for piano and violin or violoncello, no matter whether we meet them under the name of Trio, Quartett, Quintett, Sextett, Septett &c., or as Symphony, Overture, Serenade or Divertimento.

The Sonata is the pupil's most difficult task. Even with the highly-gifted the first attempts at this form are wont to prove utter failures, and it requires long study and much effort before the pupil acquires a mastery over the individual parts. The beginner however should not be discouraged by several futile attempts. If he possesses real talent for composition, if he bears within himself the corresponding ideas, he will gradually learn how to express and represent them in their correct form.

CHAPTER XII.

THE PRELUDE, ETUDE, CAPRICCIO, FANTASIA, SUITE, OVERTURE, VARIATIONS IN THE FORM OF A SONATA-MOVEMENT.
THE CONCERTO.

§ 32. The prelude as well as the Etude are as a rule pieces in simple song-form; they generally contain complete, distinctly marked subjects, this can be seen both in many of Bach's Preludes and Moscheles' and Chopin's Studies. These were previously described as "Lieder ohne Worte". Still as a rule the Prelude and Etude develop only one motive in song-form. We do not by this mean to exclude the fact that the continuation of the motive is employed as accompaniment to a melody appearing above or below it; or that the motive itself in the course of its progress may present to the ear a melody not particularly evident to the eye.

We find music-pieces under the title, Capriccio, not only in Song-form but in Dance-form and Rondo-form. We have in that case not to do with a new form; for the title only characterises the nature of the composition. In the Fantasia we also see one or several movements in a form already known to the student. Should the Fantasia contain several movements they are usually connected by some outward sign. Beethoven gives the title of "quasi una fantasia" to the Sonatas op. 27. I and II. Although in these the individual movements have no direct passages connecting them with each other, still it would be as well to perform the whole without interruption; and even where the progression from one movement to another is not indicated by "attacca", to allow only the shortest interval possible to intervene.

The Suites of the old masters contain, after a Prelude and Fugue or a Variation-movement, a number of pieces in Dance-form, between which a slow movement, "air", in Song-form, is inserted.

The strict Concert-Overture is always rendered in extended Sonata-form. Usually a long slow introduction precedes the Allegro-movement: frequently a Stretta is added to the Allegro-movement over and above the extended Coda. Most of the Opera-overtures from the classical masters retain the Sonata-form. Overtures for Oratorios are sometimes written in the form of a long Fugue for the orchestra. Mozart in the Overture to the Zauberflöte has for the most part made use of this form.

Later composers, particularly the French and the Italian, have however set aside the use of Sonata-form in the Overture. They write a Fantasia for orchestra consisting of one or more connected movements. The individual movements mostly contain subjects, which occur in the opera, but occasionally movements are met with, containing other musical ideas. As the best known and most beautiful model of such a Fantasia we would quote Weber's Overture to Euryanthe. In the latest times we often see longer or shorter Instrumental-Introductions, which have partly the character of an Introduction and are partly in Song-form. As the most interesting and melodious of this sort of introduction we would mention the "Vorspiel" to Wagner's Lohengrin.

In this book we have intentionally avoided making mention of isolated exceptions occurring in the Structure of Sonata-movements. The pupil shall and must first learn to know what is regular as a standard; later his riper knowledge will grasp why the principal subject of the movement is introduced after the Free Fantasia, in the third part, opportunely in one instance in the key of the subdominant, or totally omitted, or why in one or another instance, the Free Fantasia leads directly to the repetition of the second subject and the first subject does not appear again until later. Variations of this kind are occasionally to be met with, but in general they are so rare that we must regard them as exceptional. Besides we should have been more afraid of confusing the pupil by suggesting such exceptional cases than able to assist him.

The Concerto.

§. 33. The classical Concerto consists of three movements which almost invariably correspond to the first Allegro, the Adagio and the Finale of a Sonata. The first movement of a

Concerto presents however in many cases a difference to the Sonata-movement which we dare not leave unmentioned. Most Concertos begin with an extended orchestral introduction, which in individual instances precedes a cadence for the solo-instrument, as in Beethoven's E flat major Concerto, op. 73. Sometimes several bars for the solo-instrument, in which the principal subject of the first movement is played or introduced, precede those of the orchestral-introduction which we usually call the first "tutti"; then a long "tutti" enters, compare Beethoven's Concerto in G major, op. 58. These "tutti" usually contain the important elements of the first movements curtly and concisely expressed by the accompanying orchestral instruments. After the "tutti", the solo-instrument in conjunction with accompanying instruments begin the first part of the first movement again, but with particular regard to the representation of the solo-part.

The "tutti" previous to the first "solo" is frequently exactly in the form of the first part of a Sonata. The solo which follows, then forms a repetition of the first part. Thus, in Moscheles' Concerto in G minor, op. 58, we find the representation of the first subject in the first great "tutti" in G minor, that of the second subject in B flat major. After the close of the "tutti", a modulation is made back to G minor, after which the solo, a repetition of the first part with rich adornments in brilliant passages for the solo-part, begins.

But Beethoven proceeds differently in the first "tutti" of his larger Concertos. If we study the first "tutti" of his Concerto for the violin, op. 61, we find both the first and second subject in the key of the tonic, D major. The second subject is not produced in the dominant, A major, until the following solo. Moreover in the first tutti of his piano Concerto in G major, op. 58, the key of the dominant is not touched upon; not until the following solo does the proper second subject appear in that key.

165.   &c.

In the first "tutti" of Beethoven's Concerto in E flat major, op. 73, the keys of E flat major and minor are interchanged. The keys of the minor sixth, C flat minor, (B minor), C flat major and the dominant, B flat major, appear first in the solo. In the first "tutti" of his Concerto in C minor, op. 37, the second subject enters first in the key of the relative major, E flat major, but after eight bars we find a modulation of four bars to C major, and then the second subject appears in the latter key. The continuation and close of the "tutti" are in the key of the tonic.

From the examples cited it is sufficiently evident, that Beethoven preferred not to leave the key of the tonic in the first "tutti"; this is natural because the "tutti" closes in this key, usually upon a chord of the dominant seventh, introducing the solo which begins immediately in the same key. With Beethoven, therefore, the "tutti" does not form the first part of a Sonata-movement; it rather represents a long extend orchestral "Vorspiel" before the real first part. The important element of the first part is contained in this "Vorspiel", quite so in the C minor and Violin-Concertos, for the most part so in the G major and E flat major Concertos already alluded to.

Later composers often write only a short instrumental introduction at the beginning of the Concerto. Concertos are also to be found in which the form of the Sonata is in part or even totally abandoned. Of the latter kind is Spohr's Concerto which is in the form of a Scena. Other modern masters increase the form of the whole Concerto by the addition of a Scherzo.

The last movements of Beethoven's Concertos are generally in Rondo-form. The last movement of the E flat major Concerto, op. 73, takes the form of a simple but very extended Rondo without an episode of contrast. The Rondos to the Concertos op. 37 and op. 61 have not only episodes of contrast, but in the first part, besides the first subject, they also possess a second. This second subject together with the first is likewise reproduced after the episode of contrast but the latter does not repeat. The Rondo in the G major Concerto, op. 58, has both a first and second subject, but no episode of contrast.

The variety of musical forms in the classical works, the heterogeneousness of the representation of these individual forms is so great that it is impossible to suggest all the deviations from the original fundamental forms which are to be found scattered up and down, among the works of the great masters. The musical forms are no longer mere fixed patterns, they neither could or should be such; they are so internally connected with the subject-matter, so totally inseparable from it, that they, upon similar principles of structure, ever require and demand an admission of their manifold modifications according to the musical ideas contained within them. Has the pupil by the help of this book obtained a hint upon the analysis of the classical works, has he learnt to recognise the musical forms by their characteristics, he will no longer regard deviations in form, in the "classics", as arbitrary acts of disorder; but with unimpaired vision and a higher intellectual insight for such deviations, he will recognise them, as proceeding from the organic structure of the whole, as the Correct, the Natural and the Free, as the purest, most beautiful and most perfect arrangement in Art, and he will see the same principles of structure displayed which are clearly and unmistakeably demonstrated in the works of the masters.

INDEX.

The numbers refer to the pages.

Adagio, 2. 15. 23. 30. 40. 41. 73. 75. 89. 90. 92. 107. 149.
Allegro, 30. 89. 90. 92. 104. 139. 148. 149.
Andante, 3. 15. 50. 52. 89. 92. 107.
Aria, 30. 65. 66. 72. 73.
Art, 29. 41. 53. 64. 71. 72. 138. 152.
Bach, 1. 41. 42. 72. 73. 76.
Ballad, 30. 65. 71.
Bassoon, 52.
Beethoven, 2. 3. 4. 5. 6. 8. 10. 11. 15. 16. 18. 20. 21. 23. 25. 26. 27. 28. 30. 33. 34. 35. 36. 37. 38. 40. 41. 42. 43. 44. 45. 46. 48. 49. 50. 56. 57. 59. 60. 61. 62. 63. 72. 73. 74. 75. 77. 78. 80. 85. 87. 88. 89. 90. 91. 92. 93. 95. 96. 97. 98. 99. 100. 104. 105. 106. 107. 109. 112. 113. 114. 115. 116. 117. 118. 119. 120. 121. 122. 123. 124. 125. 127. 130. 132. 135. 136. 137. 139. 142. 143. 144. 145. 146. 147. 148. 150. 151.
Cadence, 15. 23. 24. 33. 35. 48. 50. 55. 60. 61. 81. 96. 102. 125. 146. 147. 150.
Cadenza, 90.
Caesura, 11.
Cantilene, 3.
Capriccio, 54. 148.
Caprices, 76.
Cavatina, 30. 65. 71.

Chopin, 1. 3. 11. 26. 76. 124. 148.
Clarinet, 51. 52. 139.
Clavier (Wohltemperirte), 1. 73.
Coda, 41. 49. 60. 61. 62. 71. 74. 75. 80. 84. 91. 93. 95. 96. 97. 98. 99. 101. 102. 103. 104. 106. 108. 109. 114. 115. 122. 124. 126. 136. 137. 138. 139. 142. 143. 145. 146. 147. 149.
Concerto, 10. 16. 26. 87. 90. 124. 132. 148. 149. 150. 151.
Coriolanus, 2.
Counterpoint, 129.
Courante, 53.
Cramer, 76.
Dance-Form, 53. 56. 59. 64. 77. 85. 108. 147.
Divertimento, 147.
Dominant, 11. 15. 34. 35. 37. 38. 40. 48. 51. 52. 54. 55. 70. 73. 81. 84. 85. 90. 92. 93. 94. 102. 104. 111. 113. 115. 116. 117. 118. 119. 120. 124. 128. 131. 134. 137. 139. 143. 145. 150. 151.
Double-bass, 52. 139.
Drums, 10.
Episode, 52. 73. 74. 77. 78. 79. 80. 82. 84. 85. 86. 94. 95. 104. 109. 110. 112. 113. 114. 116. 117. 118. 120. 121. 123. 124. 133. 139. 143. 144. 151.
Etude, 1. 76, 148.

Fantasia, 42. 76. 148. 149.
Fantasia, Free, 42. 65. 92. 100. 102. 122. 123. 126. 128. 129. 130. 131. 132. 135. 136. 137. 138. 143. 146. 149.
Field, 76.
Finale, 16. 45. 48. 80. 84. 85. 86. 88. 91. 107. 149.
Flute, 51. 52. 139.
Form, 42. 47. 50. 53. 54. 63. 71. 72. 87. 89. 91. 107. 108. 109. 132. 138. 144. 145. 147. 148. 149. 151. 152.
Form, Musical, 25. 63. 69.
Fugue, 5. 47. 129. 149.

Galop, 53. 57.
Gavotte, 53.
Gigue, 53.

Händel, 41. 72.
Harmony, 8. 23. 42. 43. 44. 48. 50. 68. 102. 116. 119. 125.
Haydn, 30. 41. 48. 65. 72. 108.
Henselt, 76.
Horn, 50. 139.

Impromptu, 11. 54.
Introduction, 91. 113. 115. 132. 143. 148. 149. 150.

Jadassohn, 18. 19.

Key, 4. 5. 8. 9. 15. 16. 34. 35. 36. 37. 40. 42. 46. 47. 50. 51. 55. 57. 60. 62. 66. 71. 82. 85. 93. 104. 105. 106. 107. 109. 111. 114. 120. 121. 122. 123. 124. 128. 129. 135. 137. 138. 139. 140. 141. 142. 143. 150. 151.

Lieder, 73. 76. 148.

March, 21. 54. 59. 61. 89. 108. 147.
Melody, 1. 11. 16. 23. 25. 28. 43. 44. 46. 50. 66. 69. 70. 76. 113. 131. 137. 148.
Mendelssohn, 10. 13. 27. 28. 30. 32. 41. 42. 47. 63. 72. 73. 76.

Metre, 10. 11. 35. 36. 50. 51. 54. 55. 60.
Minuet, 15. 30. 36. 40. 53. 54. 56. 57. 60. 65. 88. 89. 107. 147.
Modulation, 39. 65. 70. 85. 92. 105. 111. 114. 118. 119. 128. 132. 136. 137. 139. 145. 150. 151.
Moscheles, 75. 88. 148. 150.
Motive, 1. 3. 8. 49. 60. 61. 77. 79. 80. 81. 84. 85. 91. 93. 96. 98. 99. 100. 101. 102. 109. 112. 114. 116. 119. 120. 121. 126. 127. 128. 129. 130. 131. 133. 134. 136. 137. 143. 144. 147. 148.
Movement, 4. 5. 10. 16. 19. 30. 40. 42. 43. 47. 48. 49. 53. 54. 56. 57. 59. 60. 62. 63. 65. 66. 72. 73. 74. 75. 87. 88. 89. 90. 91. 98. 101. 102. 104. 105. 106. 107. 108. 109. 113. 115. 116. 117. 118. 120. 122. 124. 126. 128. 129. 130. 131. 132. 136. 138. 139. 140. 142. 143. 144. 145. 146. 147. 148. 149. 150. 151.
Mozart, 23. 27. 41. 42. 48. 54. 56. 57. 60. 65. 72. 86. 89. 104. 108. 140. 149.
Music, 27. 54. 66. 147.
Music, Chamber, 108. 126. 132. 147.

Oboe, 50. 52.
Opera, 65. 72. 149.
Oratorio, 65. 72. 73. 149.
Orchestra, 89. 115. 132. 149.
Overture, 2. 91. 122. 123. 139. 147. 148. 149.

Pedal, 61. 102. 113. 117. 118. 132. 134.
Period, 8. 16. 30. 33. 34. 35. 36. 37. 38. 39. 40. 44. 45. 46. 50. 51. 54. 55. 57. 59. 60. 69. 70. 73. 78. 93. 94. 112. 130. 131.
Polka, 57.
Potpourri, 42.
Preciosa, 13. 16. 31.
Prelude, 1. 76. 90. 148.

Quartett, 65. 90. 126. 132. 138. 147.

Raff, 124.
Rhythm, 4. 5. 6. 7. 8. 15. 23. 25. 42. 43. 46. 49. 52. 60. 61. 68. 69. 70. 79. 84. 129. 130. 137.
Romanza, 65. 71.
Rondo, 4. 8. 15. 30. 34. 40. 77. 78. 79. 81. 82. 84. 85. 86. 87. 90. 107. 146. 147. 148. 151.
Saraband, 53.
Scena, 65. 72. 151.
Scherzo. 3. 11. 15. 35. 54. 57. 59. 60. 63. 88. 89. 108. 147. 151.
Schubert, 2. 10. 21. 27. 28. 41. 53. 57. 66. 67. 68. 69. 70. 71. 90. 108. 123. 140.
Schumann, 5. 27. 41. 42. 63. 76. 90. 91.
Sequence 102.
Serenade, 18. 147.
Sonata, 1. 2. 3. 4. 6. 7. 11. 15. 23. 30. 33. 34. 35. 36. 37. 38. 40. 41. 42. 43. 44. 48. 49. 56. 57. 59. 60. 62. 73. 74. 75. 77. 78. 79. 80. 85. 86. 87. 88. 89. 90. 91. 92. 93. 95. 96. 97. 98. 99. 100. 104. 105. 108. 109. 111. 112. 113. 114. 115. 116. 117. 121. 122. 123. 124. 125. 126. 127. 129. 130. 133. 135. 136. 137. 138. 139. 140. 143. 144. 145. 146. 147. 148. 149. 150. 151.
Sonata-Form, 49. 91. 92. 115. 126. 148. 149.
Sonatina, 91. 92. 93. 102. 104. 106. 107. 108. 109. 122. 145.
Song-Form, 25. 29. 30. 33. 35. 37. 38. 40. 41. 43. 64. 66. 69. 71. 72. 73. 75. 76. 90. 107. 147. 148. 149.
Spohr, 20. 151.
Stretto, 80. 84. 143. 146. 148.
Study, 1. 148.
Subdominant, 15. 36. 82. 90. 105. 124. 149.
Subject, 1. 2. 8. 13. 21. 43. 44. 45. 46. 47. 49. 50. 51. 79. 81. 83. 84.
85. 91. 93. 94. 97. 98. 102. 104. 105. 109. 110. 111. 112. 113. 114. 115. 116. 117. 118. 119. 120. 121. 122. 124. 126. 127. 128. 129. 130. 131. 137. 138. 139. 140. 141. 142. 143. 144. 145. 149. 150. 151.
Suite, 53. 148.
Symphony, 1. 2. 4. 5. 19. 28. 30. 42. 48. 50. 52. 54. 56. 57. 60. 63. 64. 75. 90. 91. 115. 116. 120. 121. 123. 124. 130. 137. 138. 140. 146. 147.
Theme, 26. 28. 43. 102. 115. 129. 145.
Tonic, 11. 15. 34. 35. 36. 37. 40. 48. 50. 55. 70. 74. 78. 79. 81. 87. 90. 93. 103. 105. 106. 109. 118. 124. 128. 131. 132. 138. 139. 140. 143. 147. 150. 151.
Trio, 15. 28. 46. 48. 53. 54. 55. 56. 57. 59. 60. 61. 62. 63. 77. 85. 107. 108. 132. 147.
Trumpet, 50.
Tyrolienne, 53. 57.
Unison, 48.
Variation, 23. 30. 35. 36. 41. 42. 43. 44. 45. 46. 47. 48. 49. 51. 52. 71. 75. 107. 148.
Variation-Form, 22. 41. 43. 46. 49. 75. 147.
Verse, 27. 66. 71.
Viola, 50. 51. 52. 126.
Violin, 50. 51. 52. 56. 75. 86. 104. 108. 109. 113. 115. 116. 126. 139. 147. 150. 151.
Violoncello, 51. 52. 108. 126. 147.
Volkslied, 11. 13. 27. 46.
Vorspiel, 149. 151.
Wagner, 149.
Waltz, 53. 57.
Weber, 13. 27. 41. 149.

INDEX TO THE EXAMPLES.

The numbers refer to the Examples.

Bach, 5.
Beethoven, 3. 4. 6—16. 18. 19. 22—
24. 26—27. 30—31 a. 34—34 b. 35
—36. 38—39. 40—48. 50—53. 57—
65. 80—156. 160—165.
Jadassohn, 31 b—31 c.

Mendelssohn, 20. 41. 42.
Mozart, 17. 37. 54—56. 157—159.
Schubert, 2. 21. 66—79.
Spohr. 31 d.
Volkslied, 25. 28. 29.
Weber. 40.

www.ingramcontent.com/pod-product-compliance
Lightning Source LLC
Chambersburg PA
CBHW030253170426
43202CB00009B/729